W9-BZK-796

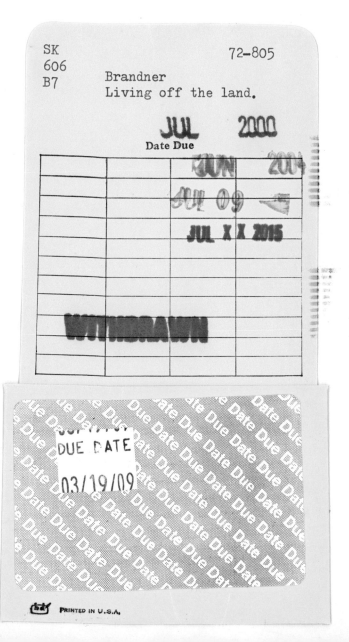

LIVING OFF THE LAND

LIVING
OFF THE LAND

Gary Brandner

NASH PUBLISHING

LOS ANGELES

72-805

Library of Congress Catalog Card Number: 77-167507
Standard Book Number: 8402-8002-5

Published simultaneously in the United States and Canada
by Nash Publishing Corporation,
9255 Sunset Boulevard, Los Angeles, California 90069.

Printed in the United States of America.

First Printing.

Contents

LIVING OFF THE LAND

Introduction

There are many books on the market for the veteran outdoorsman and the experienced camper. This book is not one of them. This book is written for the person who is inexperienced with life in the wilderness. It is written for the person who wants to sample the outdoor life to see if it has an appeal for him, and for the person who is somehow stranded away from civilization and wants only to stay alive until he can get back to the city.

The first section of the book looks at the preparations to be made for that initial foray into the wilderness. Being armed with the right kind of information, and taking along the proper equipment and clothing, can make the difference between a delightful trip and a disaster.

The middle section of the book assumes the worst—that you have become lost in the wilds or are accidentally stranded where you have no one to rely on but yourself. The chapters in this section tell how to build an emergency shelter, and where and how to get food from wild plants, fish and animals.

The final section covers some of the hazards and annoyances that everyone faces in the wilderness. Suggestions are given on how to avoid them, and how to deal with them if they occur.

At the end of the book is a list of suggested reading for the person who wants to investigate further adventures in outdoor living.

1 Be Prepared

Once you have made up your mind to sample the outdoor life, whether on an extended camping trip or just a hike through the woods, the first thing to do is sit down and think about it. You should try to plan your outing as far ahead and in as much detail as possible. It may sound like a romantic notion just to chuck it all and head for the hills, but like a lot of other romantic notions, a trip to the wilderness that is poorly planned can turn into a nightmare.

Like so many other decisions in life, one of the main determining factors is how much you can afford to spend. Although a camping trip won't cost you as much as, say, a week at Acapulco, you might as well face the fact that it's going to cost you *something*.

After you have settled on the amount you want to spend, it's time to decide where—within your allotted budget—you want to go, and what you want to do there. Next, find out all the details you can about what will be involved in your trip—things like what equipment you will need, what the conditions are for traveling where you're going, what kind of weather you should expect, what reservations you may need, and any special problems you might run into.

Getting all this advance information is not as difficult as it may sound. There are many sources available who are ready and willing to help you out.

If you have a friend who has made a trip like the one you are planning, talk it over with him. He'll be glad for a chance to show off his knowledge, and you may well avoid costly mistakes by hearing how somebody else made them.

The sports department of your local newspaper is likely to have an "outdoor editor," or at least a writer who is familiar with the camping scene. A phone call to one of these men can get you a lot of good information free.

The manager of a sporting goods store can give you some good advice on what kind of equipment you will need, but be sure you know your man. These people are, after all, in the business of selling camping equipment, and they might be tempted to load down a novice with a lot of gear he would be better off without.

There are a number of governmental agencies that can supply you with material and advice on your trip. The conservation department of the state where you are planning to go can fill you in on the laws and regulations for camping on state lands, and will tell you what permits and licenses may be required. A letter addressed to "Conservation Department" in the capital city of the state you're interested in will get to the right people.

For information on camping in national parks like Yellowstone or Yosemite, the place to write is the National Park

Service, Department of the Interior, Washington, D.C. 20240. To learn about camping conditions in the national forests, your source is the U.S. Forest Service, Department of Agriculture, Washington, D.C. 20250. Within the national forests, specific information can be had from the ranger stations on such things as trail conditions and fire regulations. The forest ranger is a good man for answering any questions you have on outdoor living.

If you are interested in camping in one of the areas that have sprung up on the large lakes formed behind dams built by the Army Corps of Engineers, your source of information is the Corps of Engineers of the U. S. Army in the state where you want to go.

For hiking trips along either of the country's two major trail systems, the Appalachian Trail or the Pacific Crest, there are private trail clubs that can answer your questions.

The Appalachian Trail consists of 2,050 miles running from Mount Katahdin in Maine to Mount Oglethorp in Georgia. Along the way are established campgrounds and shelters, along with some areas of real wilderness. The spectacular mountain scenery along the route includes the Green Mountains, the White Mountains, and the Berkshires of New England; the Catskills, the Alleghenies, the Blue Ridge range, and the Great Smokies. Information about hiking along the Appalachian Trail is available from the Appalachian Trail Conference, 1916 Sunderland Place N.W., Washington, D.C. 20036.

At the other end of the country is the Pacific Crest Trailway, which stretches all the way from Canada to Mexico in 2,156 miles of trail. This trail leads through the Cascade Range, the Sierra Nevadas, and the Sierra Madre Mountains.

These mountain ranges are higher and wilder than the older mountains of the Appalachian Trail. The place to write for advice on planning an outing along the Pacific Crest is the Sierra Club, 1050 Mills Tower, San Francisco, California 94104.

It hardly needs to be said that one all-important item in your preparation is to get maps of where you're going. First, you will want one showing the entire state or region you're going into. The familiar highway maps given away by oil companies are fine for this purpose. If you belong to an automobile club, they too can supply you with road maps and driving information.

For a map that shows all the details of the smaller area where you plan to camp, you can write to the U.S. Geological Survey, Department of the Interior, Washington, D.C. 20240. These maps show every path, creek, and peak in the area you want to know about, and can be had for about a dollar.

Maps with precise information about the national forests can be had from the U.S. Forest Service. For detailed maps of the seacoasts, the best source is the U.S. Coast and Geodetic Survey, Department of Commerce, Rockville, Maryland, 20852. The U.S. Army Corps of Engineers can supply you with maps of the navigable rivers. These are all available for a small fee.

Once you have made your plans on where to go and what to do, it is time to start thinking about your equipment. The following chapters will give you an idea of some of the things to look for, and some to avoid.

2 Tents and Bedding

There can be no all-encompassing list of equipment for campers and hikers. This is obviously because each person must equip himself on the basis of his own specific needs. Without attempting to make your list for you, this chapter and the next will pass along information about some of the things you will need, some you might want to take even though you don't absolutely need them, and a few items that you will be better off without.

TENTS

The first question you must answer when considering tents is whether you need one at all. If you're planning to spend only a single night out, and the weather is mild enough, sleeping under the stars can be a rewarding experience. If, however, you do decide to take a tent, your next problem is how much tent to take.

The simplest, lightest, and cheapest of outdoor shelters is the plain canvas tarp or shelter half. It consists of a rectangle of fabric about eight by ten feet with hemmed edges and eyelets or loops for supporting ropes. There are a number of ways that these can be pitched to provide adequate shelter for camping in moderate weather.

Shelter halves can be purchased in several different fabrics. Waterproofed canvas is the sturdiest, and will positively keep you dry in a cloudburst. It is also the heaviest and bulkiest for packing. Untreated canvas shelter halves are lighter carrying, but they will leak when rained on. This plastic sheeting is waterproof and it is cheap. However, the plastic tends to deteriorate in direct sunlight, and it tears easily once it is punctured.

If you want to go for something a little more elaborate than the shelter half, there are a number of small tents available that have the advantage of being a lightweight pack load, yet give good protection from weather and insects. One very popular model is called the cruiser tent. This one takes up about five feet by seven feet of ground space, giving enough room for two single air mattress beds. It has a waterproof sewed-in floor to keep out ground moisture, and end curtains to protect against mosquitos. Batwing flaps seal the wind and rain out of the cruiser, and a ventilator in the rear lets in fresh air when the tent is sealed up. Several smaller, one-man versions of the cruiser are also available.

Numerous other tent models are coming out on the market in ever-increasing sizes and more elaborate facilities. However, for a first try at roughing it in the woods the novice is well-advised not to go for anything beyond the trusty shelter half or one of the cruiser models.

Whether or not to go for a tent with a sewed-in floor is a

question that must be answered according to the camper's personal tastes. If living outdoors means to you being able to tramp in and out without cleaning or removing your boots, you are better off in a tent without a floor. A floor in a tent will, however, give good protection against insects, and it cuts down drafts when the weather is cold.

Despite the increased use of synthetic fibers like nylon and Dacron in tent making, most tents are still made of cotton, which includes the tough canvas and duck models. Canvas and duck tents vary in price according to their weight. The heavier the fabric is, the more protection it will give, so the more it will cost.

The high-quality cotton called balloon silk has the main advantage of being light in weight, yet still quite strong. A tent of balloon silk will stand up well through rugged use if it is reinforced at the points of strain and the seams are sturdily sewn. Don't expect tents of this cotton fabric to shed rain, though, unless they are waterproofed.

Tents made from synthetic fibers or a blend of cotton and synthetic fibers are extremely light and strong. They are, however, a good deal more expensive than cotton tents, and may not offer enough extra benefits to justify the higher price.

If you buy your tent as a package deal be sure you get all the ropes, poles, and stakes that go with it. These can easily get misplaced in handling at the store. A quality tent should have double-stitched seams and an extra thickness of fabric at the points likely to receive the most strain. If your tent is waterproofed, be sure that the solution used is nonflammable. A tent that can burn is a fearful hazard close to a stove or a campfire.

If you want to do your own waterproofing, sporting goods

stores have a variety of solutions that you can paint or spray on. Although the paint-on type of waterproofing is slower and more work than the kind in aerosol cans, it does a better job of soaking the fabric, and it is a lot less expensive.

OUTDOOR BEDDING

If you were planning to merely roll up in a blanket, stretch out on the bare ground, and sleep a blissful sleep under the stars, it's time to change your plans. For you to get a good night's sleep and awake refreshed and healthy, your outdoor bed should be warm, dry, level, and reasonably well-padded. And if there is the slightest chance of rain, you had better have a tent or some kind of shelter.

Essentially, outdoor bedding consists of an insulating material and a covering. These can be bought prepackaged in the familiar sleeping bag. Or the outdoorsman who prefers to make up his own can use a couple of woolen blankets with a square canvas tarp that he can fold to form both a ground cloth and a cover.

Any form of camp bedding is only as good as its insulating material. Waterfowl down in a sleeping bag or comforter is probably the best insulating material you can get. As you might expect, it is also the most expensive. Best of the waterfowl down is that from the arctic eider duck. Mixtures of down and crushed feathers are somewhat cheaper and somewhat less efficient.

Synthetic fibers make a light and efficient insulator that is a good deal cheaper than down, yet should be entirely adequate for the average camper. However, these days there are so many different synthetics on the market under such a variety of trade names that the buyer of a sleeping bag should be sure of what he is getting.

Good old wool is still a fine insulating material in the form of blankets for a bedroll, and it makes an adequate filler for a sleeping bag.

At the bottom of the list of preferred materials for outdoor bedding is cotton. It must be absolutely dry to be effective, and the constant thirst of cotton to collect and hold moisture is so strong that the necessary bone-dry condition is seldom achieved. The novice camper should not be misled by the low price of a cotton-filled sleeping bag nor the softness of it in the store. On the trail it will soak up not only rain, but body moisture and dew, and will stay chilly and clammy.

As for the outside cover, long-fibered cotton or light, tough sheeting of synthetic fibers or a cotton-synthetic blend will do fine. If weight is not important, a heavier fabric such as duck is even better.

Types of sleeping bag coverings to avoid absolutely are rubber, plastic, or any other completely waterproof material. A cover of this kind of material is so nearly airtight that it will trap body moisture and turn the bed into a clammy, sopping mess. The cover of a sleeping bag or blanket roll must be porous enough to allow body moisture to evaporate.

For closing a sleeping bag, a zipper that runs all along one side and across the bottom is better than one that goes only part way. This will allow the bag to be opened out flat for airing and cleaning. Snap fasteners are slower than a zipper, will not close you in as effectively and should be avoided.

A couple of sleeping bag accessories that are not considered essential by most outdoorsmen are the mattress pocket and the canopy. An air mattress placed on a ground cloth or directly on smooth ground is just as effective and a lot less trouble than inflating and inserting one into the special pocket. Also, the mattress pocket can be a dirt and trash collector on the trail. The canopy at the top of a sleeping bag is of dubious value in giving protection from the elements. At best, it may keep a gentle rain off your face for a while, but it should in no way be considered a substitute for a tent.

The most common size for a sleeping bag is about six feet long by three feet wide. For togetherness on the trail, there are some that have zippers or snaps designed so that two of them can be joined to make a double bed.

The big person, or any person who likes room to move around in bed should get the largest standard size of sleeping bag—90 inches long by 45 inches wide. Any six-footer should choose a bag at least 78 inches long. Anything shorter is likely to expose the sleeper's shoulders as he moves during the night. A roomy bag is not only more comfortable to sleep in, but it will show less wear at the seams due to strain.

If lightness, compactness and warmth are the main concern, the mummy-type sleeping bag is the best choice. The mummy bag, so called because of its tapering shape, is about 36 inches wide at the sleeper's shoulders and 24 inches or less at the feet. On some models a parka-like hood fits over the head and neck, and this feature is a very valuable one, because great amounts of body heat are lost through the head if it is left uncovered on a cold night.

Since it uses so little material, an adult-size mummy bag can be compressed into a three- or four-pound package no bigger than a football. The only drawback is the fact that some campers simply cannot get used to the bound-in feeling of sleeping in a mummy bag.

Still another type of sleeping bag is the robe style. This is essentially an oblong sleeping bag without the tough outer cover. It is light and compact, but it needs a tarp or some other tough cover to protect it from snags, sharp stones, and ground moisture.

When a separate liner is used with a sleeping bag, it increases the comfort and simplifies the cleaning job. A folded sheet of cotton flannel or light wool makes an excellent liner.

If bulkiness and weight are not problems, you can make a fine outdoor bed out of blankets and comforters you already have around the house by enclosing them in a tough tarp. Army-type wool blankets make a good bedroll. Comforters filled with wool batting, down, or Dacron are warm and comfortable. For the reasons mentioned earlier, leave the cotton blankets home.

The best pad available for the outdoor bed is an inflatable air mattress. Deflated, it can be folded into a small, neat package weighing no more than two pounds. In just a few minutes you can blow it up to form a mattress as comfortable as foam rubber.

For six-footers an air mattress of 75 inches, which is the longest standard size, is the best. The width should be at least 32 inches. A width of 25 inches is often too narrow, even for a thin camper. You can get a three-quarter length air mattress that supports you from head to knee, but this length is not favored by many outdoorsmen.

When buying an air mattress, remember that it looks somewhat longer and quite a bit wider when it is deflated. There are two main types of air mattresses: the type that consists of six inflatable tubes that run the length of the mattress, and the dimple-surfaced type that is both the most comfortable and the most expensive.

The best material for air mattresses is woven cotton or nylon impregnated with rubber. Mattresses of plain rubber, synthetic rubber, and plastics are much more vulnerable to puncture. Leaks can be repaired with a tire-tube patching kit if the mattress is rubber based, or with a plastic repair kit if the mattress is vinyl.

The preferred valves on air mattresses are the metal kind with screw tops. Push-in plastic valves are not built for rugged use.

The usual way to blow up an air mattress is with straight lung power. This takes about ten minutes. However, small hand pumps are available to do the job if you want one.

For storing an air mattress, the best method is to blow it up and stand it in a cool closet. Folding it up can cause rubber and some synthetics to crack at the creases.

A pillow is not usually considered a necessity on a camping trip, but for a person who is used to sleeping on a soft pillow at home, it can make the difference between a good sleep and a miserable night. Sleeping-bag-size pillows filled with down are available and weigh less than a pound. You can also buy air-filled pillows that weigh only a few ounces and can double as waterproof camp cushions.

The possible combinations of living and sleeping arrangements for outdoor living are limitless. This chapter has touched only on those most likely to be tried by a newcomer to camping. The following chapter deals with other camping equipment in the same way.

3 Tools and Equipment

Among people who know the wilderness best there is general agreement that the single most important tool to have along is the ax. With nothing but an ax an experienced woodsman can build a shelter, strike flint to start a fire, chop wood for fuel, cut the materials for building traps, build a raft or dugout canoe, butcher a moose or clean a fish.

As a weapon, the ax by itself is formidable, and it can be used to make a bow and arrows or a spear. A rifle that is jammed or empty is useless except as an elaborate club. The handle of an ax may break, but the head lasts virtually forever, and can be used to shape a new handle.

Although people now plan outings in the wilderness as recreation rather than a struggle for survival, the ax is still a nearly indispensable camp tool. This chapter will discuss some of the different axes available to campers, including hatchets, and a couple of other useful tools for the outdoors. Also, it will list some personal items to take along and a choice of backpacks for carrying all of it.

HATCHETS

For a short summertime stay in an established camp ground, a hatchet weighing a pound or less should be enough. A hatchet is also a good choice for hiking where the weight of the pack is an important consideration.

If you decide to buy a hatchet, you should get a good-quality one. A bargain-priced hatchet is no bargain in the long run, as the buyer usually finds he has to go back and buy a second, better one. One of the faults frequently found in a cheap hatchet is a head that is too brittle or too soft. Another is a handle that keeps working loose from the head. The extra price you pay for a hatchet with a well-tempered head and a handle that is skillfully fitted and balanced will be well worth it.

The steel in a hatchet head can vary considerably from one to another, even though they look much the same. The difference can be as extreme as the difference between the steel in a table knife and that in a razor blade. If a hatchet is to be your only chopping tool in the woods, you will want one the quality of razor blade steel.

The size and weight of a hatchet pretty much depends on what feels good to the buyer and what his needs are. A good all-around hatchet has a hardwood handle 12 inches long, a head weighing one pound with plenty of cutting area on the blade, and a squared-off butt for pounding.

Some hatchet models are made from a single piece of steel with the handle covered with some textured material for gripping. When they are properly balanced and tempered, these single-piece hatchets are excellent tools, and the handles will never break or work loose.

Hatchets in unusual styles, such as the narrow-bladed, thin-headed one that looks like a tomahawk, are not considered good choices for routine outdoor use.

A sturdy leather sheath is a must for a hatchet you will carry with you on the trail. The sheath should have rivets or an extra strip of tough leather next to the cutting edge of the blade. Belt loops on the sheath make it possible to carry the hatchet on your belt.

AXES

For outings where there will be a little more chopping, and when pack space permits it, the camper should take something a bit more substantial than a hatchet. A good choice is the model often called the house ax. This one has a fourteen- to sixteen-inch handle and a single-bit head that weighs about a pound and a half.

Axes are available in a variety of models and sizes up to the tree-felling double-bit job with a three-pound head and a handle thirty-six inches long. For the casual camper, however, nothing bigger than the house ax should be necessary, and usually a hatchet will suffice.

In buying an ax, make sure that the handle fits perfectly into the head. There should not be the slightest gap visible between wood and steel. If there is, you can be sure that someday, probably at the worst possible time, that head will fly off from that handle. Wedges of seasoned hardwood or grooved metal at the top of the handle help anchor it to the head. On some axes, a plastic sealing compound is now used to keep handle and head together.

To keep the blade of your ax or hatchet in good cutting condition, there are a few basic don'ts:

Don't chop into the ground to cut a root. Hidden rocks can nick and chip your cutting edge.

Don't use the ax to poke up the fire. That can ruin the temper of the blade.

Don't try to chop through nails, wire, or other tough metal. The ax is not made for it.

KNIVES

When picking out a knife for your trip into the woods, pass up those long, thick-bladed so-called hunting knives. Nifty as one of those may look strapped to your belt, it is just too cumbersome for most of the jobs you will want to do with a knife. Most of these will call for something smaller and more delicate.

One fine, all-around camp knife is the familiar jackknife with two slim, sharp blades. This will take care of most of the whittling, trimming, slicing, and peeling that a camper is likely to have to do.

The multi-bladed Boy Scout type knife can be a useful tool in the woods if you get a good one. It has blades designed to punch holes, drive screws, open cans, and lift caps as well as cut. In the cheaper versions of this knife, however, many of the specialized blades turn out to be sadly inadequate for their jobs.

If you feel undressed going into the woods without a sheath knife, get one with a blade no more than six inches long. For most purposes a four-inch blade is as long as you need. Avoid the long, thick Bowie knife that can weigh as much as two pounds, unless you expect hand-to-claw combat with a grizzly.

Handles of bone, wood, durable plastic, or leather rings are all satisfactory. The steel of the blade should extend all the way through the handle to keep it from breaking off.

To keep your knife sharp, it is a good idea to carry a small whetstone.

SAWS

The camp saw is a good tool to have along if you expect to do a lot of wood cutting or build a shelter. The saw is faster than an ax used by an inexperienced camper, and it is much easier to handle. Also, a saw is safer. An ax in the hands of someone not accustomed to using it can be extremely dangerous.

There are a number of good lightweight saws available that will fit readily into a backpack. One of these has a hinged aluminum frame that folds flat to form a sheath over the blade for carrying.

Another good choice is the bow saw. This one consists of a tubular metal frame in a curve similar to an archery bow that holds a thin blade taut between the ends like a bowstring. The better models of this saw have jointed frames that can be taken apart and carried in a package no more than eighteen inches long. The flexible blade can be wound up like a watch spring and tied into a small, neat package. The whole thing weighs only about two pounds, and can be quickly put together for use.

If you want a saw that is extremely light in weight, there is the model with a plastic pistol grip and interchangeable blades to cut either wood or metal. It is about ten inches long, weighs only a few ounces, and can be bought for about a dollar.

Another very light saw is a thin-bladed model in which the blade folds into the handle like an old straight razor. It is inexpensive, and can easily be carried in a jacket pocket.

The lightest of all consists of a barbed steel cable attached to steel rings at both ends. The idea is to put a finger through each of the rings and pull the cable back and forth across whatever it is you want to saw. This saw costs very little, and can just about be carried in your wallet. Don't expect super-efficiency from it, however.

COMPASSES

If your camping trip will be confined to a well-populated state park or national park, chances are you will have no use for a compass. However, if you intend to go a bit deeper into the wilds, a compass is a necessary piece of equipment.

Remember that a compass by itself will not guide you out of the wilderness or to your destination. All any compass can do is point to the north. However, a person with a good map and a knowledge of how to use his compass can get to any place he wants to go.

The most common type is the needle compass. This one has a stationary dial marked for the directions of north, south, east, and west, and graduated in degrees from 1 through 360. North is located at 360 degrees, east at 90, south at 180, and west at 270. A needle, magnetized on one end, is mounted on a pivot to swing freely above the dial. To get oriented with a needle compass, turn the instrument until north on the dial is in line with the magnetized end of the needle.

Another type of compass that is just as well suited for the camper is the revolving-dial type. This one has the directional markings and degrees printed on a pivot-mounted dial that revolves freely in the case. The edge of the dial marked for north is magnetized and always points in that direction.

The compass you select should have clear, definite markings, and should come in a sturdy case of brass or aluminum to protect it from knocks. You can get compasses in plastic cases, but they are more vulnerable to damage. A ring on the compass case is handy for fastening it to your belt for safe keeping. A fairly good compass of one of these types can be bought at sporting goods stores for about five dollars.

PERSONAL GEAR

In addition to the basic tools that are vital for getting along in the wilderness, there are some items you might get along without, but which are worth their weight in comfort and enjoyment for you.

Matches are so utterly obvious an item that they are easy to overlook. A reserve supply should always be carried by anyone going on a trip into the wilderness. The little books of paper matches are not much good in the great outdoors. It takes very little moisture to soak them to the point where they are useless, and at best they don't give enough flame to light anything in a stiff wind. Old-fashioned wooden kitchen matches are the ones to take camping. Also available are extra large wooden matches that burn for a full minute with a large hot flame, and steel matches.

Special waterproof containers that will keep your matches dry can be had cheaply from sporting goods stores. Cheaper still are a variety of tubes and boxes you probably have around the house. For instance, the plastic tube that new toothbrushes come in works well.

An important thing about a match container is that it must be easily opened. A metal can with a screw top can be jammed on the trail by sand or rust. You should be able to get the match container open easily while wearing gloves or when your fingers are numb with cold.

To waterproof your matches, dip the head and the first inch of the match into fingernail polish or melted paraffin. Prop the dipped matches up individually for about five minutes until they dry. Pack them loosely enough in the container so they will be easy to get out. Leave enough of the wood on the end of the match uncoated so that you can hold it without burning your fingers on the fierce flame.

Although you may have a dandy never-fail cigarette lighter that works just fine in the city, be warned that these gadgets have a perverse way of fouling up out in the woods. Take it along camping if you want to, but don't leave the matches at home.

A *candle* may seem like a strange item to take along on a camping trip, but its inclusion in your pack can be justified by the number of things it can do for you. First, there is light. Lanterns can break and run out of fuel; flashlights depend on batteries and bulbs that are far from foolproof. A thick candle is just about indestructible, and will give enough light inside a tent for doing routine tasks. For lighting a campfire a candle will burn long enough to dry out and ignite damp kindling that you could never get going with matches. If no other fuel is available, a thick candle under a can or pan will cook food or boil water. Put the candle inside a small can and you have a makeshift heater that will warm up the temperature in a small tent. Melted candle wax can be used to seal the seams of a leather boot or patch a small leak in tent fabric.

If you wear *glasses,* take an extra pair along when you go camping. Being without your glasses can be annoying enough in the city, but in the woods it can be downright hazardous.

A couple of sturdy *needles* and some tough *thread* are invaluable for repairing a hundred little things in the camp.

A small roll of soft copper or aluminum *wire* can be used for a great number of minor mechanical repairs. It is inexpensive, and it is pliable enough to be worked with the bare hands.

A personal *toilet kit* is a good thing to have along unless you want to come back from your trip looking like one of the sloppier citizens of Dogpatch. A small kit consisting of very few items is light and compact, and can do a whole lot to make you feel better on the trail. Following are a few recommendations for a toilet kit:

Toothbrush and toothpaste
Razor and shave cream
Comb
Nail clippers
Soap and towels
Polished steel mirror

BACKPACKS

Once you have selected the equipment you will take along into the wilderness, you need something to carry it in. There are probably close to a hundred different devices on the market for carrying equipment on your back. Only a few of them, however, are practical for our purposes.

First, and simplest, is the light *rucksack*. Essentially, this is just a sack made of canvas or other heavy material fitted with shoulder straps. It is ideal for carrying the various items a hiker will want with him on a one-day jaunt through the woods. The purpose of a rucksack is to get all these odds and ends out of your pockets and off your belt into a neat, compact package that can be comfortably carried on the back with very little restriction of movement.

You should be sure that a rucksack will carry all you want to take with you before choosing it as your backpack. If you plan to carry enough food and equipment for a trip of two or three days, the rucksack is not big enough. Likewise, if you have a lot of heavy hardware like canned goods or steel traps, the rucksack does not give enough protection to keep them from digging painfully into your back. For just a few light things, however, the thick canvas on the back of the rucksack is enough protection.

The shoulder straps of a rucksack should be leather or web, and at least two inches wide. The straps should be thick enough so that they won't curl into shoulder-cutting ropes as the weight of the pack pulls down on them. The rucksack should have sturdy buckles or snaps made of rustproof steel, bronze, or brass. Zippers and other tricky hardware to close up the rucksack are likely to make trouble on the trail.

Heavy duty canvas or duck is as good a material as any for a rucksack. The bags made of nylon or Dacron are lighter, but they lack the back protection you get from the stiffer canvas. Also, canvas is easier to waterproof and keep waterproofed than the synthetics.

A good size for a rucksack is fourteen by sixteen inches, measuring the flat back surface of the bag. The flap should be long enough to cover the bag completely when it is full. You can buy rucksacks with an assortment of outside pockets for small items. These can be handy, but two such pockets should be enough. Otherwise, you can be forever hunting through them for something.

The *Duluth packsack* is a heavy-duty rucksack with a headband in addition to the shoulder straps to help the wearer support its weight. The headband brings the powerful neck muscles into play. The main use for this type of a pack is to carry heavy loads for short distances.

For a fairly long, steady hike the Duluth pack is not the best choice. For one thing, it will keep you in a slightly bent-forward position that is not the best for looking around and enjoying the scenery. Secondly, as might be expected, the Duluth pack can give the inexperienced hiker a mighty sore neck.

The *pack basket* is a fairly rigid container made of thin woven slats of wood. When it is filled it has enough flexibility to fit the wearer's back, yet the wooden slats are sturdy enough to protect against sharp metal objects inside. The pack basket is roomy and light, and in camp or at home it can double as a storage box.

The main drawback of the pack basket is that its size cannot be adjusted to fit the load. A few things in the bottom will rattle around and drive you crazy unless the rest of the basket is stuffed with something. A bulky object such as a rolled sleeping bag won't fit inside, and is often awkward to tie on the outside because of the bulk of the basket itself.

As with all backpacks, the shoulder straps should be at least two inches wide and thick enough so that they won't curl.

The *framed rucksack* consists of a large rucksack fitted on a light frame of metal tubing. It has cross straps that hold the pack away from the body, allowing air to circulate between the bag and the back, and protecting the back from sharp metal objects.

The framed rucksack was used for much heavy-duty packing by the Army. It can carry enough gear for a seven-day stay in the wilderness. The framed rucksack has a broad strap across the hips that makes the heavy load easier to carry by lowering the center of gravity and putting a lot of the weight on the powerful leg muscles rather than calling on the back to do all the work.

EMERGENCY KIT

Although getting lost is something that happens to the other guy, it is a good idea to have a small kit prepared with emergency equipment, just in case.

An emergency kit is also a must for anyone who regularly flies over wilderness areas. For the camper, such a kit will not add a lot of weight to his regular gear, and could save his life. It is something he can take along on short forays away from the main camp while leaving his heavier pack behind.

Following are a few suggestions for equipment for the emergency kit:

Waterproof matches
Candle
100 feet of strong fishing line or copper wire
Map
Compass
Polished steel mirror for signaling
Police whistle to signal for help
Antiseptic and bandages
Emergency food such as candy bars and packets of dehydrated food
Light plastic shelter sheet, 8 feet square
Metal cup for boiling water
Light hatchet
Wool sweater
Extra pair of socks

In desert country you can substitute a canteen of water for the cold-weather clothes. You can also make other additions and subtractions to the kit according to your needs, preferences, and the terrain you are visiting.

4 Underclothing

Right at the start you should know that you don't have to go out and buy a whole new wardrobe of "camping clothes." Many times, work clothes and casual clothes you already have in the closet will do just fine. For the items you have to buy, remember that the most expensive is not always the best for your purpose.

In choosing your camping clothes you should be sure that they are reasonably sturdy, comfortable to wear, and suited to the weather you expect where you're going. Other than these basic requirements, go by whatever suits your taste and your pocketbook. Choosing camping clothes is simplified somewhat by the fact that they are pretty much the same for both men and women.

This chapter and the next two will discuss the various items of camping clothes from the skin out. The emphasis will be on the types of clothing that will be most useful for given situations, and there will be warnings against some that are impractical, inefficient, or needlessly expensive.

UNDERWEAR

For warm-weather camping—which is most camping—the best rule for underwear is just to wear whatever you normally wear at home. However, you should make certain that it is comfortable, and that it is durable enough to withstand rough use and rugged outdoor laundering.

One extra change of underwear is usually enough for any outing. If you plan to be away from civilization longer than a week, and if the weight of your pack is not important, take three sets if you want to, but that's an extravagance. Setting up a small camp laundry in warm weather is no problem, and you can wash one pair while you wear the other. A man's cotton shorts and undershirt will dry overnight or in a couple of hours in the sun. If you're only going out for a day or so, just take the underwear you have on.

Cotton is about as good a material as you can find for summer underwear. Wool has certain advantages in dispelling perspiration and it doesn't get a clammy feel when wet, but it is too warm for summer in most climates, and it can feel scratchy and irritating next to perspiring skin. Besides, woolen undergarments are a good deal more expensive than cotton.

Shorts and undershirts made of synthetic fibers such as nylon or Dacron are very light and strong and fast-drying, but they have a flaw as far as their use on a camping trip is concerned. These man-made fibers are much coarser (when looked at closely) than nature's, and when they are woven into a fabric they can be painfully abrasive. This is especially noticeable when pack straps rub an undershirt against bare skin over miles of hiking. And those light nylon shorts that you hardly know are there in the city can scrape you raw in a few hours of walking in the woods. Most of the things you will do on a camping trip will involve a lot of movement and, therefore, friction. Because of this, underwear made of smooth cotton or fine wool is your best bet.

When the weather gets nippy in the fall, or if you plan a trip to higher altitudes, you will need longer and heavier underwear than the cotton shorts and T-shirt that were good enough for a warm-weather hike. One- or two-piece sets of cotton underwear with long legs and sleeves will do the job in temperatures down to freezing, as long as the weather is dry and calm. In damp coastal areas where there are strong winds, more body heat will be drained off at forty or fifty degrees than in dry areas where there is no wind and temperatures are as low as twenty degrees.

Another effective type of underwear for chillier weather is the so-called "thermal" underwear. The "thermal" quality consists of a method of weaving the fabric into a waffle-like pattern of protrusions and hollows. The pockets in the cloth next to the skin trap air and form an insulation against the rapid escape of body heat. But a word of caution—the term "thermal" as used for this type of underwear does not mean it has any magical heat-producing capability. It merely means that this type of cloth will keep you warmer than the same weight of cotton cloth in a tight, flat weave.

The same benefits and limitations apply to the currently popular fishnet style of underwear. Undershirts and shorts of this style are made of soft cords woven with large gaps between them. These gaps, when covered by outer clothing, form insulating pockets of air in the same manner as the hollows in thermal wear. The warmth afforded by fishnet underwear, along with its lightness, make it quite acceptable for cool-weather outdoor wear. The excellent ventilation through the large open spaces allows free evaporation of body moisture.

Also, net underwear worn without an outer garment has been found to be cool and comfortable for hot-weather wear. It lets in enough sun to give you an even tan. However, it is well to remember that net underwear does not have the power to keep you cool in a blistering heat wave, or warm in a blizzard.

An especially good type of underwear for fall and light winter camping is the two-layer style with an inner liner of cotton under a suit of wool. The thin cotton layer is smooth and comfortable against the skin, and will not scratch as wool often does. The outer layer of wool and the layer of air trapped between give this type of underwear an excellent ratio of warmth-to-weight. Also, body moisture can escape without causing the cloth to become clammy.

In cold winter weather the inexperienced camper is more likely to get in trouble because he wears too much underwear than too little. The fall-weather underwear already mentioned is completely satisfactory for ordinary winter conditions. When overly heavy underwear is worn during exertion, such as an arduous climb or a stretch of snowshoeing, it can become uncomfortably hot. When this heavy underwear becomes wet with sweat, it turns wretchedly cold when the hiker stops to rest.

For exertion in cold weather, the best combination is light wool, cotton net, or two-layer underwear worn under warm and windproof outer garments that can be easily opened or taken off before sweat forms. When at rest, the camper can replace or close up the outer garments, thus staying reasonably comfortable all the time.

There are situations, however, that call for extra underwear protection such as two suits of wool or long johns insulated with some synthetic fiber. When a person is motionless for a considerable length of time, such as a hunter in a duck blind, extra warm underwear is a necessity. And anyone out in temperatures of zero or below can use the added warmth.

A specialized type of underwear is that called "insulated." These are quilted suits that have a layer of fluffy insulation sewn between two layers of thin woven fabric. The insulating material is usually a synthetic fiber, but some expensive suits stuffed with waterfowl down are available. These suits have a bulky look, but are actually quite light in weight. This type of underwear holds in enough body heat to allow the wearer to use less bulky outer garments. Insulated underwear is especially good for long periods of intense cold when the wearer does not move around much.

The danger with insulated underwear is that it may be too warm for normal outdoor exertion. Underwear that becomes soaked with sweat quickly turns into a frost trap when the wearer stops to rest.

It is important to be sure before investing in insulated underwear that you actually need its extra warmth. When buying this underwear you should see that the outer cover and inner lining are a soft fabric, that the quilting is well-stitched, and that the insulating material is not some unnamed "miracle" substance.

SOCKS

The best choice in socks for all-around outdoor wear is top-grade wool. These are warm in the winter and cooler in the summer than thinner fabrics that trap perspiration. Wool socks also have a soft, springy texture that is your best protection against blisters. They also dry quickly when wet. Other types of socks may wear longer, but top-grade wool is durable enough to survive routine outdoor activities quite well.

It should be remembered that all wool socks are not the same. The cheaper wool socks are likely to be loosely knitted or to be made of wool with short, brittle fibers or of reprocessed wool. Socks like these are no bargain because they wear out fast. A single day of hiking in the mountains can put your heel through the fabric.

However, top-grade wool socks will last for months of rugged wear and many launderings, staying soft and comfortable. These are made of fine, long-fibered virgin wool, and the knit is close enough so the fibers will not pull apart when the sock is stretched. Natural or bleached white wool is preferred over colored wool. Although most of the dyes used to color socks are safe, some might cause an allergic reaction or an infection in a broken blister.

Proper fit of the socks is of prime importance. They must be snug enough not to bunch at the toes or heel, and they must be tight so that they slide down into the shoe or boot. The socks should be long enough to reach three inches above the ankle if they are to be worn with low shoes. If they will be worn with high shoes or boots they should reach two inches above the boot top.

The best bargain in socks for rough outdoor wear is the blend of wool and synthetic fibers. They are cheaper than top-grade wool socks, and they last longer. The higher the percentage of synthetic fiber in the blend, the longer the socks will last. However, this increased durability comes at the cost of some of the softness, warmth, and ventilation of top-grade wool. For the hiker who is literally a tenderfoot, it is a good idea to choose socks with a percentage of synthetic fiber no higher than forty percent. For an outing in mild weather where not much walking is planned, socks of sixty percent synthetic and forty percent good wool will do the job.

Socks made entirely of synthetic fibers are less expensive than either top-grade wool or the wool-synthetic blends, and they last virtually forever. These are adequate for trips that won't involve much hiking or very hot or cold temperatures.

Cotton socks are the least expensive of all. The main drawback of cotton socks is their tendency to collect moisture and become soggy. However, if you're planning a leisurely outing where your socks can be kept dry, cotton is very comfortable.

When the temperature dips below freezing, the choice of socks becomes much more critical. Wearing the wrong socks in these conditions can result in frostbite, which can cause the loss of toes, feet, or even life.

If you plan hiking in subfreezing temperatures, two pairs of socks worn inside leather boots are a good choice. The inner pair should be high-grade wool, soft and fluffy for comfort. The outer pair, which gets most of the friction against the boot, can be a tougher blend of wool and forty to sixty percent synthetic fiber. The inner pair of socks in this combination need be no longer than ankle height. The outer pair should extend two inches beyond the top of the boot.

If you plan on long periods of immobility, such as sitting in a duck blind or fishing through the ice, a third pair of socks can be worn for extra warmth, as long as they don't cramp your foot inside the boot, cutting down circulation.

Insulated socks are now available that have a loose insulating material such as down, wool, or synthetic fibers quilted between two thin layers of fabric. These socks are very warm, if somewhat bulky. A light inner sock worn under these will make them more comfortable.

Socks made of thick, porous rubber are good for outings where there will not be too much moving around, as they do an excellent job of holding in the body heat. However, they are not recommended for hiking or other strenuous outdoor activity since they trap perspiration from the feet and quickly become clammy and uncomfortable.

5 Outer Clothing

Once you have taken care of the clothes that go next to your skin, it's time to think about your outer garments. Remember that it is not necessary—probably not even desirable—to go into the woods looking like an ad for Abercrombie and Fitch. In choosing suitable clothes for camping, looks are pretty far down on the list of things to be considered. Far more important are comfort, durability, and correctness for the climate where you are going.

TROUSERS

When you buy trousers for outdoor wear, the most important consideration is that they fit right. This is not as obvious a requirement as it seems. Many women have a tendency to buy trousers that are too tight to allow freedom of movement, or even enough space to breathe in properly. Men, for some reason, often buy trousers that are too short at the waist and too long at the cuff.

An easy rule to remember for getting the right waist size for both men and women is to buy camping trousers one inch larger than the size you wear at home. This will leave room for heavier underwear and thicker shirts. If the pants are still a bit loose, a good belt or a pair of suspenders will solve the problem of keeping them up.

Another place where you should allow an extra inch or so is in the measurement from the crotch to the top of the trousers. This will give you more freedom for the energetic leg movement required for hiking in the woods. Also, it leaves room for thicker underwear and the extra items campers often like to carry in their pockets.

There is no valid reason for having long cuffs on outdoor trousers. Cuffs that come all the way down to the heel get damp and muddy if the weather is wet, and can easily catch on snags and rocks in the trail. Turned-up cuffs are bad too. They too easily can hang up on brush and snags and trip the hiker. Also, turned-up cuffs quickly soak up moisture and are great collectors of dirt and trash. Men who make their living working outdoors wear their cuffs fairly high—at the top of the ankle or even higher when they wear high-top boots.

Because of the hard wear they get, outdoor pants have to be especially durable. The seams should be reinforced with cross-stitching at points where the strain is greatest. The fly should have a sturdy zipper or hefty buttons that are sewed on with tough thread. You should have deep and roomy pockets for the many small things you will want to carry with you. Suspender buttons on the trousers are a good idea, since suspenders are better for supporting the load of full pockets than a belt is.

There are pants available with facings of plastic or leather, which are fairly expensive. You would be well advised to avoid these unless you plan to do a lot of wading through thorn bushes. They are unnecessarily heavy for most outdoor wear, and are hard to keep clean.

The best style of trousers for camping is a plain slack design with no pleats, no built-in belt, and no cuffs or other useless fripperies. The seat and legs should be loose enough for freedom of movement, but not so loose that they will flop around. Hold your pants up with suspenders, a strong leather or web belt, or both if you plan to really load your pockets. This trouser style will do for both hot and cold weather. If the weather is cold or wet, merely use a heavier, warmer fabric.

Trousers with snug-fitting knitted cuffs may look sporty on the dummy in the store window, but they are a poor second in the woods to loose cuffs worn outside the shoe. Although they have some value in added warmth in cold weather, knitted cuffs are too warm for the summertime, and they are liable to cause unnecessary friction in hiking.

The tucked-in cuffs also funnel rain water down into the shoe instead of spilling it off outside the way loose cuffs do. In the same way, the tucked-in cuff helps fill the shoe with dirt and bits of twigs, while the fuzzy knitted part is a great grabber of burrs.

Tight, form-fitting jeans are popular and they are tough, but they have a couple of drawbacks that make them not the best choice for camp trousers. First, they are cotton, which makes them unsuitable for wet climates or colder temperatures. Also, jeans have tight pockets that are not easy to get into, and their snug fit is not especially suited for the trail.

Traditionally, the best outdoor pants have been made of wool. In recent years, however, the development of new synthetic fibers has produced fabrics that are equal, and in some cases superior, to wool. The synthetics are more durable than wool, and usually less expensive.

Wool is still an excellent choice for very cold weather, and lightweight wool is fine in the summer too. A blend of wool and synthetic fibers can be quite satisfactory, as long as the workmanship is good.

For mild weather such sturdy cotton fabrics as denim and duck work well. The stiffness these have when they are new can be softened up by washing. Remember, however, that nearly all cotton pants shrink some when they are washed. Be sure that yours still fit before you set out on the trail.

Corduroy pants are neither warm enough nor sturdy enough to justify their bulkiness. They tend to blot up moisture, and they are slow to dry. Corduroy pants are fine for a picnic in the park, but for anything more rugged they cannot be recommended.

SHIRTS

There are a number of things to look for in buying a shirt for outdoor wear. First, the shoulders and sleeves should be roomy, and the tail should be long enough so that it won't pull out when you're hiking. Pick long sleeves in preference to short ones. Long sleeves give protection against weather and insects, and when it's mild you can always roll them up. With short sleeves you're vulnerable to cold, sunburn, and mosquito bites.

Roomy breast pockets in a shirt are always useful. They should have flaps that button closed to keep the contents in and the twigs and trash out.

Your outdoor shirt should have large strong buttons sewed on tightly. Zippers are never entirely foolproof, and one that jams out in the woods is next to impossible to repair.

As far as color goes, there is something to be said for nearly all of them except black and white. Black absorbs too much heat in the summertime, and white shows the dirt too readily. If there is liable to be hunting nearby, a bright red or yellow shirt will hopefully distinguish you from a deer. If the only animals you expect to run into are four-footed, a soft shade of tan or green is less likely to startle them.

A sturdy weave of cotton is as good a material as any for a warm-weather camp shirt. The synthetic fibers are also acceptable for summer as long as the fabric is pliable and fairly soft. A top-grade wool shirt is fine, and it will dry fast if it gets wet, but a wool shirt will cost you about twice as much as one of cotton or synthetic fibers. Wool is also harder to clean, and it won't wear as long as the others.

In colder weather, however, good wool shirts are your best bet. Good surplus army and navy wool shirts are available at low prices and are warm and durable. Look out, though, for imitations that are khaki or navy blue in color, but are not true service surplus. These can be of shoddy quality and uncomfortable against the skin for any length of time.

SWEATERS

A loose, long-sleeved, soft wool sweater is an excellent item of clothing to have along on a camping trip, and can be carried easily in the top of your pack. When your shirt is not quite warm enough, but a jacket would be too much, a sweater will fill the bill perfectly. It is also useful for sleeping in if you're caught without enough bedding, and rolled up it makes a fine pillow.

Inexpensive sweaters of wool or synthetic fiber are quite suitable for routine camping. The cotton sweatshirt-type sweater is all right as long as the weather is dry and no colder than freezing, but it is of very little use when things get wet or extremely cold.

COATS AND JACKETS

The good old army field jacket is quite acceptable for outdoor wear in cool, dry weather, and it can be bought for a very few dollars in sporting goods and surplus stores. If it gets very cold or wet, though, the field jacket is inadequate. It is too thin to hold in much body heat, and water quickly soaks through it.

Canvas hunting jackets, like army field jackets, are all right as long as the weather is not too extreme. The good ones will shed a lot of rain and keep out the wind, but they won't keep you warm unless you have some heat-holding clothing on underneath. Canvas coats with a double thickness of fabric at the shoulders and sleeves are especially good for fending off the rain.

Leather jackets, which have a certain fashion value in the city, are all right for outdoor wear, except that they are just too expensive for the purpose. You can get jackets that give you the same warmth and protection for a lot less money.

Mackinaws, the thick, thigh-length wool coats, are an excellent choice for normally cold weather. Even though they get damp with rain or snow, the thick material of the mackinaw holds in body heat, and it dries in a hurry. The length is ideal for protecting most of the body without getting in the way of knee action or dragging in the mud when the wearer stoops or bends down.

One drawback to the mackinaw is its weight and bulk. Quilted coats filled with down or a fluffy synthetic are much warmer for their weight, and just as good at keeping you dry. These will cost up to twice as much as a wool mackinaw.

If you're wearing insulated underwear or a wool shirt and sweater combination, a tightly woven parka of synthetic fiber is efficient and very light. The nylon or Dacron jacket is windproof, sheds rain and snow reasonably well, and wears like iron. Again, this combination of insulated underwear, wool shirt and sweater, and parka are more expensive than the trusty mackinaw.

The best coat available for wearing in extreme cold is one quilted and insulated with waterfowl down. If you're headed for below-zero temperatures, and price is no hindrance, this is the coat for you. A quilted coat stuffed with fluffy synthetic fiber will cost a bit less, and will be a bit less warm. A coat lined with fleece or alpaca pile is warm and wears well, but it is very heavy and bulky, and can cost a high price.

CAPS AND HATS

The billed, or baseball-type cap is a good all-around piece of camp headgear. When it comes in wool with earflaps it will keep your head warm in temperatures down to zero. One problem with this type of cap is that it lets rain water trickle down the back of your neck when a shower hits. This can be avoided by wearing a hooded parka with the cap.

The wide-brimmed, cowboy-style hat is good protection in all kinds of moderate weather. It will shade you from the sun and keep the rain off like an umbrella. The woven straw models are good for hot, dry weather. It is a good idea to wear a chin strap with the straw models as they have a tendency to blow off your head.

For very rainy weather the fisherman's oilskin with the extended brim in back is as good a hat as any. For rough weather, get the model with earflaps and chin strap.

The traditional sun helmets of pith or cork are unnecessarily heavy and awkward compared to visored cloth caps that give just as much protection.

GLOVES

There are more uses for gloves on a camping trip than keeping the hands warm. The hands of the average city dweller can quickly become a mass of burns, scrapes, and scratches in routine camp work, no matter what the weather is. Gloves are also better than insect repellant for protecting the hands from mosquito bites. Lightweight cotton work gloves are a sensible precaution for the novice camper whose hands haven't been toughened in the woods.

Thick wool gloves will keep your hands warm in temperatures down to freezing. Leather gloves lined with wool are good down to zero. If it gets any colder than that, mittens are better than gloves, but they make working more awkward.

6 Footwear

Since the condition of your feet is of prime importance to your comfort and even your survival outdoors, you will want to give special attention to your selection of footwear.

The most important consideration for camping shoes should be the material that most of the shoe, other than the sole and heel, is made of. There are three basic materials in which outdoor shoes and boots are available:

1. Leather, for the best all-around quality
2. Rubber, for constant wet traveling
3. Canvas, for non-rugged outings

Leather is usually the best choice, as it can handle any kind of outdoor going except a lot of water. In buying leather footwear you should be sure that the leather is pliable and has a uniform texture. Your best safeguard against inferior shoes is to buy a brand you know from a store with a good reputation. A tip worth remembering is that shoes of flawed or inferior leather can often be disguised by dyeing them black or dark brown. It is easier to see the quality in leather that is not darkly dyed. A good quality outdoor shoe will be smooth, pliable, and slightly moist with a sheen of oil. Steer clear of shoes that have the shiny look of a polished dress shoe.

As mentioned, leather is not highly resistant to water. Processes that claim to "waterproof" leather help somewhat, but they often have the unfortunate side effect of sealing the pores that allow the leather to "breathe" and dissipate perspiration from the feet.

If you expect exceptionally wet going, rubber boots are the best choice. When they are insulated, rubber boots also do a good job of keeping out the cold.

Canvas shoes, such as sneakers and tennis shoes, are cheap, light, cool, and won't skid on precarious footing. On the other hand, they don't offer much protection from cold or wet, and they are not very durable.

Although leather is the preferred material for the main part of the shoe, stay away from outdoor shoes with all-leather soles and heels. These slide around easily, soak up moisture, and wear out fast.

Rubber or a tough synthetic material make the best soles and heels for all-around outdoor wear. The rubber sole with cords or fabric embedded in it is good too. These soles are durable, tough, flexible, and they won't slip on normal surfaces. Also, rubber or synthetic soles do not soak up water, and they cushion the shock of walking on hard surfaces.

The best method of closing up outdoor shoes or boots is with tough rawhide or nylon laces through open eyeholes. On high-top boots, hooks speed up the job of lacing, but they are not foolproof. Cheap hooks can rust, bend, and break.

Oversized hooks can get snagged on the brush. A zipper is easy and quick as long as it is in good working order, but zippers are subject to jamming in outdoor wear, and once jammed they are nearly impossible to repair in the woods. Boots with buckles across the top of the foot may be stylish, but they fit too loosely for any strenuous outdoor hiking.

You can buy a lightweight rubber boot that contracts to fit snugly at the ankle after you pull it on. This style is more convenient for walking than the stiffer, higher rubber boots.

TENNIS SHOES

The light canvas-topped, rubber-soled shoes called sneakers or tennis shoes are fine for a casual outing where you won't be doing much walking over rough country or through swampy land. If you get them big enough so that you can wear two pairs of fluffy athletic socks inside them, tennis shoes will keep your feet warm in temperatures down to freezing. The chief advantage of tennis shoes is their cost, which is the lowest of any acceptable outdoor shoe, but they are not recommended for long jaunts as they give the foot very little support.

G.I. SHOES

The homely G.I. shoes available at low cost in surplus stores make an excellent outdoor shoe for most camping wear. They have plenty of space in front for your toes, and the low, flat heel gives good balance. The rubber soles provide a sure-footed grip, and the ankle height and lack of lining allow good ventilation. The best type of G.I. shoe for camping is the one with the rough side of the leather on the outside, and a plain toe. Those with a hard, box-type toe may take a better shine, but they are more likely to rub blisters on your foot. And a shoeshine is of little value in the woods. The so-called "paratrooper" boot with a high top and buckles is just excess clutter for the camper, who will hardly ever need boots with tops any higher than eight inches.

BIRDSHOOTER BOOTS

The light, sturdy leather boots with a seam completely encircling them from the top of the toe around behind the heel are called birdshooter boots. The seam is the cause of one of the problems with this kind of footwear—it tends to become scuffed and worn where it crosses over the toe in the course of hiking. Many birdshooters are made with unnecessarily high ten-inch tops. Seven or eight inches is a better height for most campers. The soles should be rubber or composition, and the shoes should have eyelets instead of open hooks. A heel that is tapered at the front is good for shedding mud, and it will not catch as easily on rocks and roots as a heel with a squared-off front. A platform sole with a single surface from toe to heel is good too.

HIGH BOOTS

Aside from their rather romantic lumberjack appearance, laced leather boots that reach to just below the knee have little to recommend them for general outdoor wear. First, it is a lot of extra bother just lacing them up. Then the constriction of the tight boot around the calf cuts down on circulation and can bring on muscle cramps. The high tops also sag down and cause chafing around the ankle and heel. If all you want is some snapshots of yourself looking sporty and outdoorsy, go ahead and lace on a pair of high boots. But if you're serious about tramping around in the woods, pass them by.

RUBBER-LEATHER COMBINATIONS

A popular form of outdoor footwear is the boot with a rubber bottom sewed to a leather top. These go by a number of different names, one of which is "shoepacs." These are excellent footwear for wet and cold weather. When the tops are well greased they are almost as waterproof as all-rubber boots, and much better ventilated. When they are worn with two pairs of socks, shoepacs will keep your feet warm in temperatures down to zero. They are reasonably priced, and they wear well. As with other boots, the tops should be no higher than you need. The leather tops should be greased with some product that won't damage the rubber. For all-around wear shoepacs are not considered to be as good as all-leather boots because the feet will sweat more in the rubber bottoms when the weather is warm, and the looser fit around the ankle is not as comfortable for hiking.

COWBOY BOOTS

It should be sufficient to say that cowboy boots are best left to cowboys. For any other type of wear, including camping, they are a mistake.

SKI BOOTS

Like cowboy boots, ski boots are fine for their designed purpose, skiing in this case, and that's it. For any other kind of outdoor wear they are far too stiff, heavy, and awkward.

INSULATED BOOTS

There are on the market a couple of styles of insulated boots. One is rubber with the foot and sole insulated by some material such as felt between two layers of rubber. Another is leather with the insulating material sandwiched between the outer leather covering and the liner.

The rubber insulated boots are waterproof and plenty warm, but the feet may get damp and clammy during a long stretch of hiking. Also, if the outer layer of rubber is punctured the insulating material soaks up water like a sponge, and it becomes a real chore to dry it out.

Insulated leather boots can be even more trouble. In any kind of wet going, water will come through the leather and quickly soak the insulation. They are also heavy and hot in warm weather. In most cases a couple of pairs of socks inside regular footwear will be better than insulated boots, and a lot less expensive.

ALL-PURPOSE FOOTWEAR

No single type of outdoor footwear will suit everybody all the time, but for the camper who wants a single pair of outdoor boots or shoes that will carry him through various conditions of weather and terrain, the following can be a useful checklist.

Upper Material: Should be middle weight unlined leather, not waterproofed or insulated.

Soles and Heels: Rubber or tough composition material.

Height: Not more than seven inches.

Size: Roomy enough for an extra pair of wool or wool-and-synthetic socks in cold weather.

Closure: Rawhide or nylon laces run through rustproof eye rings.

Wet Weather Provision: A light coating of oil or grease will keep these shoes dry through light showers. For wetter going a pair of heavy-duty low rubbers pulled on over the shoes will do the job.

7 How Not To Get Lost

Getting lost in the wilderness, as we shall see in later chapters, is not the end of the world. All the same, it is no fun, so the wise man who heads out into the wilds will take steps to see that it doesn't happen to him.

The first and most obvious precaution is to stick to the trail. All trails lead *somewhere*, and you are a lot safer following one than striking out on your own through the brush. However, since you can't always stay on well-traveled paths, there are some other things you can do that will help keep you from getting lost.

If you plan to rely on "instinct" to get you where you want to go, or to bring you back to where you started from—forget it. There is no such thing as an instinctive sense of direction in man. A veteran outdoorsman who seems to find his way through "trackless" wilderness by instinct is really going by the sun, the wind direction, the slope of the land, the way the vegetation grows, and a dozen other natural direction finders that the tenderfoot wouldn't notice. Traveling over country he is familiar with, the woodsman notes these indicators without consciously thinking about it.

Tests conducted by the Army have shown that it is virtually impossible for a man to walk in a straight line without some indicator to guide him. In the tests men with all degrees of outdoor experience were blindfolded and told to walk on a straight line in an open plain. The blindfolds kept them from seeing the sun, and there was no wind during the tests. Either of these would have given the men a clue to directions. The results were that every man tested walked in a circle, some to the left, and some to the right, but always in a circle. These tests only confirmed what has long been known to veteran woodsmen—no man can steer a straight course without some navigational aids.

Luckily, the average person who wanders off the trail, or becomes otherwise disoriented in the wilderness will not be blindfolded, and he will not be on a featureless plain. There will be many natural direction finders available to him if he knows how to use them.

What good, you may ask, does it do to know what direction you're traveling in if you don't know where *you* are? By itself, none. However, knowing which way is north, say, and keeping oriented will make it possible for you to walk in a straight line. If you walk far enough in a straight line, you will walk out of the woods. If you move in circles you are lost for sure.

A compass is, of course, the best way to keep headed in a straight line. Unfortunately, too often a compass is not available to the man who suddenly finds himself disoriented. Lacking a compass, the sun is a reliable guide, traveling as it does a regular daily route from east to west.

On a clear night the North Star (Polaris) traditionally points the way for voyagers. Fortunately, you don't need a course in astronomy to be able to locate the North Star. Every schoolboy can point out the constellation of seven stars that make up the Big Dipper. And once you have found the Big Dipper, finding the North Star is easy, because the two stars that mark the front end of the Dipper's bowl point directly up at it.

The sun and stars, good direction finders though they are, are useless when hidden behind a blanket of clouds. The direction the wind is blowing may be of some help to a man familiar with the territory. However, the tendency of the wind to shift around makes it an unreliable indicator for a novice.

One method of walking in a straight line, even in a driving rainstorm, is to locate two landmarks on a line in the direction you are walking. Move toward the nearest one, keeping both landmarks lined up ahead of you. When you have almost reached the first, pick out a third, more distant, landmark on a line with the first two. Keep up this procedure and you will stay headed in the same direction. Always be sure you pick out the third landmark before you actually reach the first.

If you are forced to detour from your straight line by swamps, cliffs, or other natural hazards, pick out a landmark behind you on the line you are traveling. When you are able to return from your detour, walk until your landmarks are lined up as before, then continue on your original course.

Spending a little time studying the maps of your region before you go in can be a great help in not getting lost. If you fix the main features of the territory in your mind you won't have the feeling of being in an utterly unfamiliar place. A map can give you an idea of the pattern of roads and trails in the area, how far they are from each other, and in which direction.

If there are tall peaks in the area a map will identify them. It will show you if there is a major stream and where it leads. A map will locate swampy areas and impassable cliffs that could force you to detour from your course. Any lookout towers on the major peaks will show up on the map. All this and much other useful information can be had just by going over a map beforehand and making an effort to remember some of its salient features.

When you head out into unfamiliar territory where there is a lot of tall uncut timber, you can do much to avoid trouble finding your way back by paying close attention to your route and marking your trail. From time to time you should turn around and check on the landmarks behind you. They are the ones you will be seeing on your way back. Count how many ridges or streams you cross and make a mental note of the number.

If you are following a trail, mark the correct route each time you take a fork. An arrow scratched in the dirt will do the job nicely, and will last for days. For a more permanent marker, you can cut a small blaze on a tree or break an occasional twig or small branch along the way. The white inner wood of a broken twig will stand out plainly against the dull natural colors of the forest around it. Make special note of any unusual features of the woods along your way. These serve as natural markers to look for on your return trip.

One overrated piece of direction-finding lore that many of us remember from boyhood is the notion that the side of a tree trunk with moss growing on it is north. In a general way, this is probably true, but there are enough variables to make it a poor method for the inexperienced woodsman to use. The growth of moss on tree trunks can be influenced by such things as the prevailing winds and nearby bodies of water. In swampy areas with heavy rainfall there is often as much moss on one side of a tree as the other.

8 Don't Panic

For the person who takes all the precautions outlined in the preceding chapter, it is almost impossible to get lost. His route will be carefully planned, his trail marked, and a map and compass ready at hand for checking will keep him constantly informed of his exact position.

Unfortunately, in the real world most of us are simply not going to be that well prepared. When the sun is warm, the breeze fresh, and the woods ahead of us green and inviting, there is little time for pessimistic thoughts of getting lost. This is one reason why many thousands of people get lost every year.

For the majority of people who lose their way in the wilderness, the most critical moment is the point at which they first realize that they really are lost. The way in which a person reacts to this frightening realization is crucial to his well-being and his survival. It is at this instant that a slight irritation or a vague feeling of puzzlement about what happened to the trail gives way to the scary words, "I'm lost!"

It is here that the most dangerous beast of the wilderness is apt to strike. The beast's name is Panic. Of all the casualties among people lost or stranded, by far the largest percentage is the result of panic. The forest that had looked so inviting is suddenly dark and forbidding. The fresh breeze turns chill, and the sun seems to plunge toward the horizon, trailing darkness behind it like a black banner. There is a feeling of being utterly and completely isolated.

Panic brings with it an almost uncontrollable urge to push on, to hurry, to run as though a burst of frantic activity might bring you to safety.

Actually, such rushing off in all directions is probably the worst thing you can do when lost. Nine times out of ten such a blind dash to escape will only get you more thoroughly lost.

An important thing to know is that this feeling of panic is not unnatural. Anyone lost in the woods for the first time will feel it. It is the reaction to the panicky feeling that makes the difference. The novice camper should know that he is vulnerable to panic, and he should also know that if he gives into the irrational urge to flee he will only put himself in deeper trouble.

The first thing to do the instant the word "lost" hits your mind is to stop traveling. Take off your pack. Sit down for a while. If you're a smoker, light up. If you have something with you to eat, get it out and have a bite. Perform any other little actions you can think of that will keep you in the same spot until you get over the urgent need to hurry.

It is often a good idea at this time to start a fire. A good crackling fire can be very calming and reassuring, and can give a person the feeling of having a camp right where he is. When you have relaxed somewhat and have shaken off the early symptoms of panic, you are in a much better mental condition to start thinking about getting yourself out.

In your mind, retrace the steps that brought you to your present position. Try to remember the last time you were still definitely on the right track. Many times the mistake you made will pop into your mind with sudden clarity. It might have been a wrong fork you took in the trail. Perhaps you kept a stream on your left that should have been on your right. Maybe you took the wrong slope down from a ridge. After you have busied yourself with distractions like having a smoke and building a fire, it will be much easier to think your way back to safety.

If the answer does come to you clearly and positively, put out your fire, pack up your gear, and be on your way. However, if you have even the faintest doubt about your course, mark your trail so you can find your way back to this spot where you first stopped to get your wits together. That way you will at least be no worse off than you were before.

If mentally retracing your steps does not make your mistake clear to you right away, don't leave the little camp you have set up. If you have a map and compass, get them out. Look for a recognizable landmark, a river or a peak. Locate it on the map. Determine in which direction to go to reach a trail, and how far it is.

If you don't have a map or a compass, try drawing as much of a map as you can remember. Draw it in the dirt with a twig if you have no pencil and paper. If nothing comes of that, climb a tree and have a look around for anything familiar. If there is a rise nearby that will give you a vantage point, climb that. But be sure and mark the trail behind you.

Listen for any familiar sound that will help you get oriented—the rush of water, traffic noise, the sound of an ax biting into wood.

If none of this does any good, plan on spending the night where you are. Make yourself as comfortable as possible, and plan on attacking the problem early in the morning. If the stars are out, locate the North Star and mark its direction for use the next day.

A different set of problems from those of the camper who strays off the trail or wanders away from camp face a man unexpectedly stranded out in the middle of nowhere. An airplane can go down in the wilderness. A jeep or dune buggy can conk out somewhere on the trackless desert. The other fellow, the one you were relying on to get you where you were going, can fall victim to an accident or sudden illness, leaving it suddenly up to you to get out.

Almost always, when stranded in real wilderness, it is a better idea to stay put than to try to travel. A downed plane is much more easily spotted from the air than a man on foot. In the desert a stranded vehicle can be seen for a long distance. Unless you know a short, certain way out, stay with your vehicle.

An exception to the stay-with-it rule is the case of an airplane down in tall, dense growth such as a tropical jungle. A downed plane can be completely swallowed up by this type of growth, making it invisible from the air. The tops of trees close over the wreck, leaving no sign that the jungle has been disturbed.

This solid roof of vegetation also makes signaling with a mirror useless and breaks up smoke signals. If there is a clearing nearby the survivor can set up there for signaling.

Otherwise, he would do better to make for the coastline or a major stream or river. Floating downstream on a raft is probably the surest way to get out of a tropical jungle wilderness.

Remembering a few basic facts about being lost in the wilderness can do a lot to ease the pain of the situation. Here are a few things to keep in mind:

1. By far the greatest danger of being lost is the unreasonable panic that causes people to exhaust or injure themselves in mindless rushing around.

2. The woods are almost always a safer place—if you are calm—than the streets of a city.

3. Wild animals—bears, wolves, and such—if any exist in the woods you're in, will be more than willing to leave you alone if you do the same for them.

4. Most cases of people "getting lost" in the temperate climates happen only a few miles from a good trail or road that will lead them swiftly to safety.

5. Even a person stranded in extreme climatic areas such as the deep desert or the arctic stands a good chance of surviving if he keeps his wits about him, puts up a good shelter, and uses emergency signals efficiently.

9 Finding Your Way Out

After building your fire and spending your first night lost in the wilderness, it is time in the morning to launch some positive efforts to get yourself out. This does not mean you should be in any hurry to leave your temporary camp. If you were with other people who might be searching for you now, build up your fire with green branches and get a healthy smoke going. Do some scouting around your camp, being careful to stay in sight of your smoke, or marking your trail back. If you have a good piercing whistle, let one go now and then, or do some yelling to attract any searchers who might be within earshot.

If you have a gun with you, three shots fired at intervals of about five seconds are recognized as a standard distress signal. So are three fires built to send up three separate columns of smoke.

When you leave your temporary camp on forays to hunt for the trail, leave a message behind to tell the searchers where you are in case they happen on your camp while you are gone. Move around carefully when you do leave your camp, keeping your eyes and ears open.

If you have no compass and you didn't check the North Star the night before, note the direction from which the sun rises, mark that as east, and get yourself oriented accordingly. Often a little unhurried scouting around in the morning will show you where you are and solve a problem that seemed overwhelming the night before.

If it is not likely that anyone is looking for you nearby, you can say goodbye to your emergency camp and strike out on your own. In many regions well-traveled roads and trails are no more than ten miles apart. If this is the case where you are, all you need to do to get out of the woods is walk in a reasonably straight line.

When you abandon your camp, you should still leave a message for anyone who comes upon the remains of your fire. Tell which direction you headed in and what time you left.

When you are ready to go, douse your fire, pack all your gear neatly, and set out in the direction you feel will take you most quickly to a road or trail. There are a few pointers that can help you make a fairly good guess about which way to go. For instance, if you spot a long, low ridge that runs through the forest for several miles, chances are it will have a trail on it. In rough country a trail will usually follow the line of least resistance, and a low ridge will provide steady and fairly level going.

If your choice is between traveling uphill and downhill, head for the lowlands. A creek is a good guide to take you downhill toward civilization. Trails often follow along creeks and rivers. However, if there is no trail right alongside your waterway, don't make it hard for yourself by plowing along right next to the bank where the ground may be swampy and the brush especially thick and tangled. Instead, follow the general course of the water by moving along a trail or across open country on top of a low ridge or along the side of a hill above the stream.

Don't feel you have to follow a stream or river if you know there is a road or railroad track that you can reach in a shorter and easier stretch of traveling across country. The bends and loops made by a river, especially where the country is fairly flat, can double the distance of straight-line travel to your destination.

The best way out of a thicket, swamp, or plains region without natural passages such as rivers or ridges is to follow a straight-line course. You should choose the direction that is most likely, on the basis of what you know for sure, to lead you to a settlement, road, river, or railroad. Keeping on a straight-line course is easiest to do when you are following a compass. If you are without a compass, the sun can give you a general course, or you can use the lined-up landmark method of following a straight line that was described in Chapter 7. In a swamp or dense thicket, this can be a frustrating and slow way to travel, but it will keep you from walking in circles. A patch of thicket only a couple of miles square might as well be the Amazon jungle for a person who is walking in circles. There are few experiences more demoralizing than the sudden realization that you have passed this same spot before.

One note of caution is worthwhile on straight-line travel. It is not uncommon for a man to be so intent on his personal navigation that he hikes right past some obvious guidepost, or even right across a road or trail without noticing it. Your straight-line progress, whether you're using a compass or lined-up landmarks, should be slow and methodical with plenty of pauses to look around and scan the area for signs of civilization or familiar objects.

A person who is confused about which direction to travel should follow the first man-made trail or travel route he comes to. These include any kind of a road, a pack horse route, a blazed trail, or a line of telephone poles or power poles. Any of these will eventually lead to a larger road, a settlement, a camp or some sort of human habitation.

It is worth mentioning again that in following any of these routes, your best choice is downhill. Villages, houses, and most major roads will be found in valleys. Heading uphill will almost certainly take you deeper into the wilderness.

10 Signaling For Help

Sometimes the kind of terrain a person is lost or stranded in is too rough or dangerous for him to try to walk out. Or an injury could leave him unable to hike. Maybe he is simply too confused to travel with any assurance. In any of these cases the surest and quickest means of getting rescued is the proper use of signals.

A person who knows how to make the correct use of emergency signals will nearly always be picked up in short order. Spotting aircraft are available all over the country, and rescue helicopters can go in just about anywhere and bring someone out.

One important thing to remember about emergency signals is that many of them are based on the number three. Three gunshots are a distress signal that is recognized all over North America. Three fires laid to send up their smoke columns in an even row are another. Three blasts on a whistle will call any help that is within earshot. The international Morse code distress signal, SOS, is tapped out with three dots, three dashes, and three more dots.

RADIO

If you are stranded with a downed airplane or stalled vehicle that has a radio, that is the first thing to try. Even if you don't know how to operate the instrument, fiddle around with the dials and switches if there is any chance that it is still operative. Any kind of transmission you put out, no matter how garbled, may be picked up and lead rescuers to you.

MIRROR

The signal mirror has been said by rescue pilots to be second only to the radio in attracting attention. A pocket mirror or any shiny piece of metal or glass can beam a signal that is effective up to ten miles on a clear day. Signal flashes from the ground are easily seen from a plane flying many thousands of feet high.

Survival kits sold in surplus stores contain a mirror designed specifically for signaling. This type of mirror makes it possible to aim the beam of reflected light exactly at a target. The signal mirror comes with a hole in the center in the shape of a cross. To use the mirror you sight through the hole at your target, such as the cockpit of a searching plane. Reflected on the rear of the mirror you will see a spot of sunlight on your face where the sun shines through the hole. Tilt the mirror then to line up the spot of sunlight on your face with the hole in the mirror. Keep sighting through the hole at your target. This will aim the beam of light where you want it to go.

A bright piece of tin with a hole punched in the center can serve as an improvised signal mirror, and is used in the same way. For the best chance of attracting the rescuer's attention, move the mirror so it produces flashes in series of threes.

FIRE

During the day, the essential thing about a signal fire is that it give off a lot of smoke, the denser the better. One good way to smoke up a fire is to feed it with green or damp vegetation. Grass is good for this purpose as are evergreen boughs. If there is oil or rubber available from your disabled vehicle, these will help your fire produce a heavy black smoke. Try out whatever materials you have at hand.

As we noted, three fires in a row are a recognized signal of distress. If there is not enough fuel available for three fires, puffs of smoke can be sent up in groups of three by trapping the smoke in a blanket, Indian fashion. You will need a good smoky fire for this trick, and it won't work on a day when the wind is blowing.

At night the brightness of the signal fire is what counts, since the smoke cannot be seen in the darkness. This is the time to feed a signal fire with dry wood and material that produces the biggest, brightest flame.

A signal fire should always be built in the most conspicuous spot around that is handy both to your camp and a good fuel supply. An open beach, a clearing, or the top of a ridge are good locations. Tall trees over a fire will hide both the flames and the smoke from rescuers.

FLAGS

In an area of dense vegetation a person on the ground can be impossible to see from a plane. In a case like this, attention can be attracted by three flags tied to the top of a tall tree. Any white or bright colored clothing can be used for the flags. The taller the tree they are hung in, the more likely it is that your signal flags will be seen.

FLASHLIGHT

If you have a flashlight or lantern it can be used at night from a high vantage point to spell out an SOS call for help. This is done with three short flashes, three longer flashes, and three more short flashes. If you are not sure in which direction your light is most likely to be seen, try it in all directions. If you have neither flashlight nor lantern, you can improvise one by cutting open one side of a can and putting a candle in it. You can block off the light momentarily with your hat or a piece of cardboard to produce signal flashes.

WRITTEN MESSAGE

In some areas like sand, snow, or level grassland, a message like "HELP" or "SOS" can be spelled out on the ground. The important thing in attracting attention is that the letters contrast with the background. On snow or light sand the letters should be dark. On dark ground the letters should be light colored.

In snow, dark clothing or evergreen branches can be used to form the letters. If the snow is deep enough for shadows to provide a contrast a message can be stomped into it. On a dark background pieces of white clothing or peeled branches show up well. Always make the letters as big as you can.

11 Emergency Shelter

Once it becomes clear that you are lost or stranded in the wilderness, it is time to think about providing a shelter for yourself. Your chances of surviving will be greatly increased, and your physical discomfort reduced if you have an adequate shelter. For a lost or stranded person, shelter and enough sleep rank in importance with food and water. Loss of sleep will exhaust you as quickly as lack of food.

You should look around for a place to make your camp at least two hours before sunset. The first step is to decide what you need to make yourself as safe and comfortable as possible, then look around for them. The following are items to consider in selecting a place for your emergency camp:

1. The availability of good drinking water
2. Available food
3. Ground that is level enough for your bed
4. Protection from wind and cold
5. Available material for your shelter and bedding
6. Absence of insects
7. Available firewood

A man lost in the woods is not likely to happen upon a wilderness paradise with all these advantages, but the more of them he can find, the better off he will be.

Try to make your camp with as little expenditure of time and energy as possible. Remember that a narrow valley or a ravine between steep hills collects cold, heavy air at night, and it will be several degrees colder then the high ground. A natural terrace, a clump of thick brush, a shallow depression in the ground, or a good-sized rock on the side of a hill away from the wind will give you the beginning of a shelter.

Before settling down, take a good look around your site. Check any caves or crevices in the rocks for snakes, and examine hollow logs for ticks or stinging ants that could make your night miserable.

To provide for warmth during a cold night when you are without blankets, the first thing to do is get a good fire going. Lay the fire in an area about six feet long by two feet wide. Keep it going well for a couple of hours while you busy yourself with other chores such as gathering materials for your shelter and bedding. After this time the ground underneath the fire will have absorbed heat that will stay there most of the night. When you are ready to turn in, push the burning wood and hot coals of the fire three or four feet to one side and clear and smooth the area where the fire had been for your bed. If there is loose sand or mineral dirt around, an inch or so spread over the area will help hold in the warmth.

LEAN-TO SHELTER

The most simple shelter to put up, and therefore the only one you will likely be interested in building under the circumstances, is the lean-to. The lean-to consists of two fairly sturdy poles leaned against a thick log, or a low branch, or a boulder, or anything else that will get one end of the poles at least three feet off the ground. The poles should be about six feet apart.

Next, attach cross bars to the two poles in ladder-rung fashion. The more of these you can find and attach, the sturdier your lean-to will be. When the framework is complete, cover it with evergreen boughs. The needles of the boughs should be pointing downward, and the boughs should be put on from the ground up and overlapped like shingles.

If the lean-to is to protect you from a heavy rain, the roof must be three or four inches thick, and the slope can be no flatter than 45 degrees.

EVERGREEN BOUGH BED

You might as well be prepared for the fact that your unplanned night in the wilderness is not going to be one of the most comfortable of your life. However, there is a lot you can do with available materials to make it more comfortable than trying to sleep on the bare ground. A mattress of evergreen boughs, for instance, is sweet smelling and springy, and could be quite enjoyable if you weren't lost. There is, however, a right way to make a bough bed, and just piling up a bunch of branches isn't it.

Not that you need any particular skill to put together a bough mattress, but it takes about an hour to do it right. First, gather enough evergreen branches of the right size, which is eighteen to twenty inches long. Lay the branches in rows with the stub ends toward the bottom of the bed, or stick the stubs diagonally into the ground. The under surfaces of the branches should be downward. Lay the boughs in rows six to eight inches apart for the length of the bed. The bed can then be covered with the fine, feathery tips of other branches. To best keep your bed of boughs together, lay it inside a frame of small logs or rocks. You will sleep inside this frame.

Young fir or balsam trees make the best beds. Spruce, hemlock, and pine are also good.

SNOW SHELTERS

If you are unlucky enough to be stranded in snow country, the main job your shelter must do is break up the movement of air and hold in the heat of your body or your fire. To do this the shelter should be small, windproof, and as nearly enclosed as you can make it. The smaller the air space is around your body, and the less the air circulates, the warmer the shelter will be. One snow shelter that meets these requirements and is simple to construct is the snow cave. The best place to build a snow cave is where there is a firm crust on the snow, or where the snow covers low-hanging evergreen branches. Here you scoop out a hollow so that the crust or branches form a roof.

If you build a fire, a more open shelter is necessary to

guard against carbon monoxide poisoning. In this case, a trench in a low snow drift or bank will do. The floor of the trench can be lined with boughs, and more boughs placed across the top for a roof. The roof should be made strong enough to support a layer of snow. The fire should be built at the entrance. A reflector of boughs, logs, or snow blocks can be arranged to reflect the heat inwards.

If you do not have a fire, close off the entrance. Don't worry about air. Enough will filter through to you. If you can keep your body insulated from direct contact with the snow, and prevent the air from circulating, you will stay reasonably warm.

DESERT SHELTERS

In the desert the most important considerations are protection from the sun and heat. These make shelter in the desert almost as critical as in the snow country.

Your primary protection from sun and heat is your clothing, so resist the temptation to take it off. A layer of clothing over as much of your body as possible helps protect you from sunburn, fends off hot air, and acts as a wick to aid in the cooling evaporation of sweat.

A place in the shade away from the direct sun is greatly to be desired. If possible, stay in the shade of your disabled car or airplane. This will also help rescuers find you. Otherwise, try to find natural shade such as vegetation, overhanging rocks, or a dry wash. As a last resort you can dig a trench in the sand deep enough to shade you from the sun as you lie in it during the heat of the day.

If you doubt that finding a patch of shade is worth the effort, consider that an area of solid shade on the desert will be up to thirty six degrees cooler than the same area baked by the unscreened sun.

When no shade is to be found, the area a foot above the ground will be about thirty degrees cooler than it is at ground level. Anything that will elevate you, like a cot or a thick bed of brush, will let you be much cooler than sitting or lying on the bare ground.

The emergency desert shelter will be for your use during the day, since the nights cool off considerably, and it is then that you should work or travel. Tests performed by the military have shown that a man can travel twice as far at night on a given amount of water than he can by day. According to their experiments, a gallon of water can take a man twenty miles in the desert night, while he could get only ten miles to the gallon moving in the daytime.

12 Drinking Water

The single most important factor in determining the survival of any person living off the land is water. In moderate weather the average adult needs from one to two quarts a day to operate efficiently. A person who does nothing but rest quietly can live for five days in 100-degree temperature without water. If he exerts himself his life expectancy goes down to three days. In temperatures between fifty and seventy degrees a normally healthy man may live ten days without water. However, the dehydration of his body will leave him weak and helpless long before he dies.

FINDING WATER

In most wilderness areas a person should not have to walk too far before he finds some body of water—a spring, a creek, a lake. In arid desert regions, however, the problem of finding water becomes much more critical.

A good way to start the search for water is to scan the countryside for any patch of vegetation that looks greener or lusher than the rest. In desert areas such a patch of vegetation will usually be found at the bottom of a valley or canyon, or at the base of a hill. Often, these signal the presence of a desert spring. These springs may seep back into the earth within a few yards of where they come out, but the vegetation around them will be a clue to their location.

Without the greenery that signals a spring, the desert traveler can either follow a well-traveled game trail, or just keep heading downhill, following the runoff channels of the rare desert rains.

Any road or trail with signs of human travel is likely to lead to water more quickly than the other methods. Well-used game trails that lead toward a hollow usually indicate that there is water there. From a good elevation these trails can be seen from great distances radiating from the water source like the spokes of a wheel. Following the downhill route will lead to water ninety-nine percent of the time, but there is no way of telling for sure how far away it is.

Digging for water in the sand of dry desert stream beds can be written off as a waste of time and effort. Such areas where water can be reached by digging with hand tools are so rare that any newcomer to the desert has next to no chance of hitting one. The water under most of these dry waterways is probably twenty feet down, and a thirsty digger would be dead long before he got to that depth. A much better course is to follow the dry stream bed downhill in hopes of finding a depression where water may still be pooled on the surface.

The barrel cactus, so called because of its shape, can be a

source of water. This cactus is found in the deserts of the southwestern United States. To obtain the water, cut off the top of the cactus and mash the inner pulp against the sides. The water will ooze out and collect inside the bowl of the cactus.

Beside a stretch of ocean beach where there is no fresh-water inlet, a hole dug in the sand below the high water mark when the tide is out will collect any fresh water seeping toward the ocean. The fresh water will fill the hole before the heavier salt water seeps in from the sea.

Snow and ice are, of course, ready providers of fresh water in cold country. All you have to do is melt them—in your mouth if you don't have a fire and container available for the job.

One source of water that is always fresh and safe to drink is rain. Rainwater can be collected by spreading a sheet of fabric, such as a waterproof coat, so that it forms a funnel into a container. A hole scooped in the ground can collect rainwater if you scrape little drainage ditches leading toward it. The fine soil in many desert areas will hold rainwater long enough for the mud to settle without losing too much through seepage. If the water in your hole is draining out too quickly through porous soil, drink it at once, mud and all.

PURIFYING WATER

Even where finding water is no trouble, and there are many lakes and streams around, the unhappy truth is that it is likely to be polluted and dangerous to drink. This is especially true of any water that has flowed through an area inhabited by humans. There are a number of things you can do to make reasonably sure the water you have found will be fit to drink.

Boiling is the most common method for purifying water. To kill any possible dangerous germs the water should be boiled for at least five minutes. Boiled water, though pure, has a flat taste that can be improved by shaking it up vigorously to get some air back into it. Another way to temper the flat taste is to sprinkle a little salt into the boiled water.

Another way to quickly kill any germs in water that is suspect is to use halazone tablets. They are very inexpensive, and can be bought in most drug and sporting goods stores. Two tablets of halazone will purify a quart of water in about half an hour.

Iodine tablets for water purification will do the same job in about the same time. Lacking the tablets, you can use two or three drops of tincture of iodine in a quart of water. In about thirty minutes the water will be safe to drink.

If the water is discolored or muddy you can filter it by pouring it through several layers of clean fabric or through fine sand. The more fabric or sand you use, the better the job of filtering. Although the filtered water will be cleaner, it still isn't purified. The water should still be boiled.

NATURALLY PURE WATER

Fresh spring water dipped at the point where it bubbles out of the ground is almost always pure. The farther the water has to run, particularly through country where it is accessible to men, the more likely it is to be contaminated. Still pockets of water formed by slow-seeping springs are, however, likely to be polluted.

Lakes and streams in the high country are far more likely to contain water pure enough to drink than are those in the lowlands.

Taking a drink of polluted water may do you no immediate harm at all, as shown by the fact that thousands of people consume the stuff every day. However, some of the deadly diseases carried by germs in the water make drinking it straight a risk not worth taking. Some of these diseases are amoebic and bacillary dysentery, cholera, typhoid, not to mention parasitic worms. A good rule to follow about drinking water is: *When in doubt, boil it.*

13 Wild Plant Food

After water. the most important item for survival in the wilderness, or anywhere else, is food. For the man who is lost or stranded, wild plants are a valuable source of nourishment. This chapter will give you an idea of what to look for in the way of edible plants, which parts make the best eating, and some plants to stay away from.

Actually, there are not nearly as many poisonous plants and fruits in the woods as many city dwellers suspect. There are three rules that you can follow to avoid most of the wild plants that are poisonous.

1. Don't eat any unfamiliar plant which has a fruit, stem or tuber filled with a milky white fluid.

2. Don't eat any strange plant food that burns or stings the mouth when a sample taste is taken after it is cooked.

3. Unless you *know* edible mushrooms from poisonous ones, don't eat any of them.

SINGLE LEAF PINE NUT   WALNUTS

BLACK OAK ACORN   WHITE OAK ACORN   CHESTNUT

NUTS

One of the most nourishing of all wild plant foods, and among the most widely distributed, are edible nuts. All nuts can be eaten raw, but the taste of some is improved by boiling or roasting.

Pine nuts are the seeds from the mature cones of pine trees. They are about the size of the tip of your little finger, and are very tasty and nourishing. The best producers of edible nuts are the single leaf pine, the sugar pine, the pinon pine and the Coulter pine. You don't have to distinguish between the different pines, just shake or break the seeds out of the cone and try eating them.

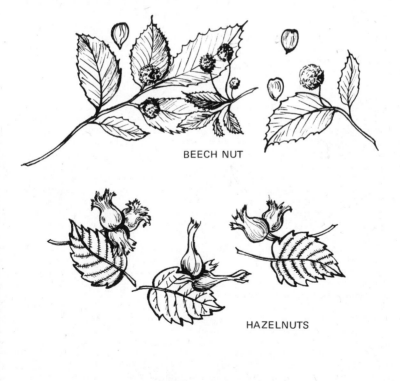

BEECH NUT

HAZELNUTS

Acorns are the round, capped nuts that grow on a variety of oak trees and shrubs. Sweet acorns can be eaten raw. Others have a bitter taste and are more palatable boiled or dried and roasted. Acorns can also be ground into flour.

Chestnuts grow on trees or shrubs similar to oaks, and have a spiky covering with a soft, leathery lining.

Walnuts grow wild in two varieties: the black walnut and the butternut, also called the white walnut. The black walnut grows on a large, wide-spreading tree with rough, dark brown bark. The nut is enclosed in a tough spherical husk two to three inches in diameter. The butternut grows on a tree very similar to that of the black walnut, except that it is not so large, and the bark is a lighter shade of brown. The nuts grow in clusters on the ends of branches, and they are elliptical rather than spherical in shape.

Hickory nuts grow on tall, wide-spreading trees with rough, shaggy bark. They grow with a husk that, unlike walnuts, is sectioned and splits off to leave the nut free. Hickory nuts are light tan in color, about an inch long and an inch wide and slightly flattened to about three-quarters of an inch thick.

Hazelnuts grow in clusters on small trees or bushes. They are covered with a leaf-like husk.

FRUITS

Apples are seldom thought of as a wild food, so accustomed are we to thinking of them as growing in cultivated orchards. However, wild apples of all sizes and colors are found in the woods of the northeastern United States.

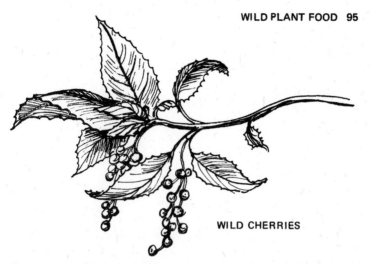

WILD CHERRIES

Although these don't make very good eating raw, especially when unripe, they can be tasty when cooked. Crabapples grow in a number of varieties throughout the country. Like other wild apples, they are better cooked than eaten raw.

Wild cherries are found on trees and bushes throughout the United States in the summer and fall. They are smaller than the cultivated kind, being about 1/2 to 3/4 inch in diameter. Their color when ripe ranges from red through brown to black. Chokecherries are about the size of a pea, and are too astringent for easy eating raw.

The *papaw* is a tropical type of fruit that grows in many forests of the United States, principally along streams. The fruit is four or five inches long with a greenish-yellow skin that turns brown a few days after the fruit is picked. It has a sweet, yellow pulp with a taste somewhat like a banana. The tree is small and slender, usually not over twelve feet high. When papaws are ripe they fall from the tree, so the best ones are gathered from the ground.

Persimmons are unfairly known for their astringent, mouth-puckering quality, which they have only when they

PAPAW

are green. The ripe fruit is a dull orange in color, and is quite soft and sweet tasting. Persimmons ripen in late fall and early winter, when the ripe ones can be shaken from the tree.

Wild grapes grow in most parts of the country on climbing vines, and ripen in the fall and winter. There are many varieties of wild grapes, most of which are sweet and tasty when they are ripe.

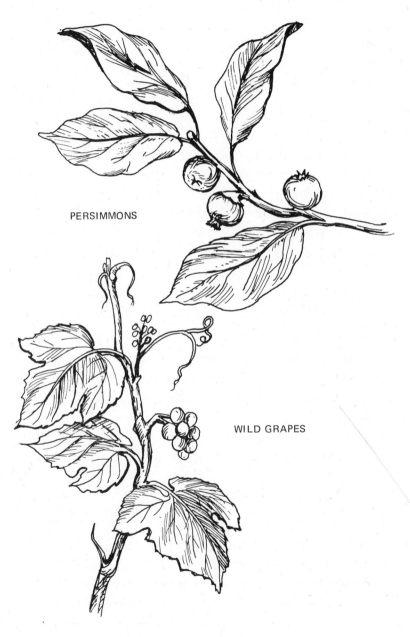

PERSIMMONS

WILD GRAPES

BERRIES

The *juneberry* is a small, purplish berry that grows on small trees in the eastern part of the country. Another variety, called the serviceberry, grows in the Pacific Northwest and in northern California. Other types of juneberries grow on knee-high shrubs in mountainous areas.

Mulberries are dark purple in color when ripe, and grow from the Eastern Seaboard west to beyond the Great Plains. They are most easily gathered by placing a sheet beneath the tree and shaking the ripe berries into it.

Currants grow on low prickly shrubs throughout the forests of the United States. The berries are tasty when eaten raw or cooked.

Wild blackberries are one of the most numerous of wild fruits. They ripen in midsummer, and are found mostly in fairly open land or on the edges of forests.

Wild raspberries grow on bushes two to five feet tall, mostly in the northern part of the country. South of the Great Lakes, wild raspberries are found only in mountainous regions. They are smaller and somewhat tastier than the cultivated kind.

Elderberries are fairly abundant, and are not hard to find and gather. They grow in clusters on the ends of branches, and ripen in August or early September. Although they are not the tastiest of wild berries, elderberries are especially nutritious, being one of the richest natural sources of Vitamin C.

Blueberries and *huckleberries* (the names are often used interchangeably) are found in most parts of the country growing on shrubs of various sizes. They ripen throughout the summer months, and are often abundant on burned-over forest land.

Wild cranberries are related to blueberries, and are found primarily in the northeastern section of the country. Wild cranberries are not easy to find because of their low, inconspicuous bushes and the fact that they often hide in peat bogs.

Wild strawberries are generally conceded to be the most delicious of all wild fruits. They are most abundant in the northeastern United States, though there is a variety that grows on the Pacific Coast, mainly in the mountains. Wild strawberries are small and not easy to pick, but their delicious taste makes it worth the effort.

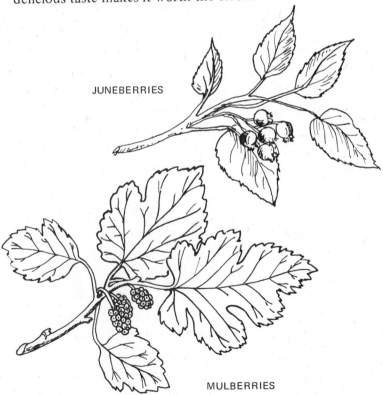

JUNEBERRIES

MULBERRIES

ELDERBERRIES

WILD RASPBERRIES

BLUEBERRIES

ROOTS AND OTHER UNDERGROUND PARTS

Wild onions are one of the most widespread and abundant of all wild food plants. One form or another is found in every state from the Atlantic to the Pacific, and from Canada to Mexico. The surest way to recognize a wild onion is to take a sniff. The aroma of onions is unmistakable. The bulb of the wild onion can be eaten either raw or boiled.

Spring beauties are well known as a lovely five-petaled wild flower. Not so well known is the fact that a bulb on the end of their roots, two or three inches below the plant, is highly edible. They can be eaten raw, or cooked in any way you cook potatoes. The taste is something like potatoes, but sweeter and more flavorful.

Water chestnuts, though more common to Asia and some Pacific islands, grow wild in some freshwater swamps of the United States.

Water lilies have a fleshy rootstock that, along with the tubers, is edible and fairly nourishing raw or cooked. However, on some varieties the rootstock is too bitter to be palatable without long cooking.

Wild potatoes and *sweet potatoes* grow wherever the climate is fairly warm. They can be baked, roasted, boiled or fried, and the leaves and stems can be eaten as greens.

Arrowhead is a plant similar to the wild potato. It grows all year around in wet ground or shallow water. The edible bulb is found at the end of a thread-like root.

Bulrushes, which grow all year in wet and swampy areas, have roots and a white stem base that can be eaten raw or cooked.

Cattails provide food not only from their starchy roots, which can be eaten baked or roasted, but from the white portions of the new shoots and the buds from the flowering spikes. If possible, any part of the cattail should be eaten hot, as it is much tastier that way than cold. Cattails are found in most parts of the country, always near water.

Wild rice, which costs you a buck for a few ounces in the supermarket, can sometimes be found among the tall grasses along swampy rivers and streams. The lower stem and root shoots are sweet and tasty when chewed, after you have removed the tough outer covering. The grain is delicious cooked. The stem and root shoots are best in the spring and summer; the grain in late summer and fall.

WILD ONION

SPRING BEAUTY

WATER CHESTNUT

ARROWHEAD

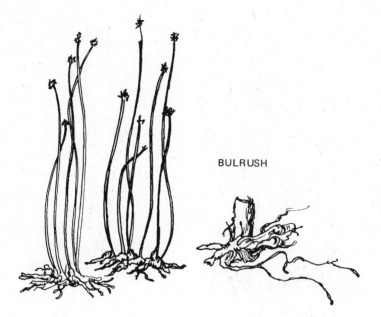

BULRUSH

WILD POTATO

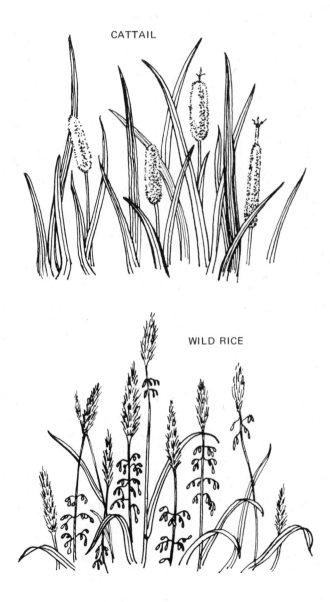

CATTAIL

WILD RICE

LEAVES, STEMS, AND SHOOTS

The *burdock,* which grows seemingly everywhere and snags onto your pants legs, provides a delicately flavored vegetable in its tender leafstalks, peeled and eaten raw or cooked. Burdock roots, although they are a considerable chore to dig up, are edible too.

Goosefoot, sometimes called pigweed, is ordinarily one of the most unwelcome of weeds. It grows everywhere, mostly in the spring and summer. As emergency food in the woods, the cooked greens taste much like spinach. The seeds can be roasted and eaten too for added nourishment.

Plantain is another weed common to most parts of the country in the spring and summer. The young leaves of the plantain can be boiled or eaten raw.

Purslane, the ground-hugging plant recognizable by its fleshy green leaves, is a prized vegetable in several European countries. In the United States, where it grows wild in rich, sandy soils, it is considered only a stubborn weed. In the woods the leaves, stems, and flower buds can all be cooked with savory results.

Dock is still another common weed that can provide food for a person lost or stranded in the wilderness. The young leaves can be eaten raw or boiled.

Dandelion leaves provide some of the tenderest and most succulent greens available in or out of the woods. Also, the roots can be eaten raw or roasted and broken up to provide a workable coffee substitute.

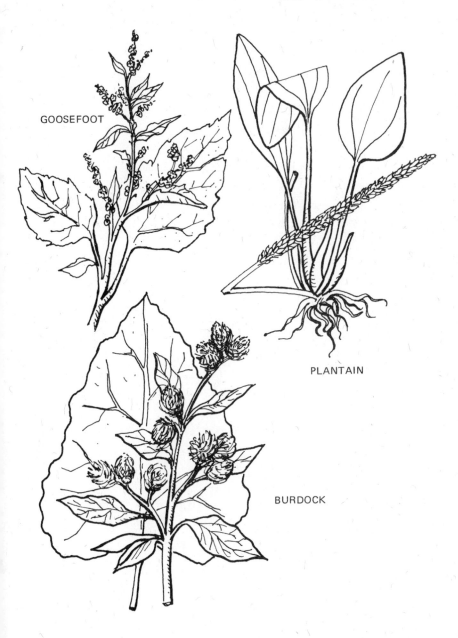

GOOSEFOOT

PLANTAIN

BURDOCK

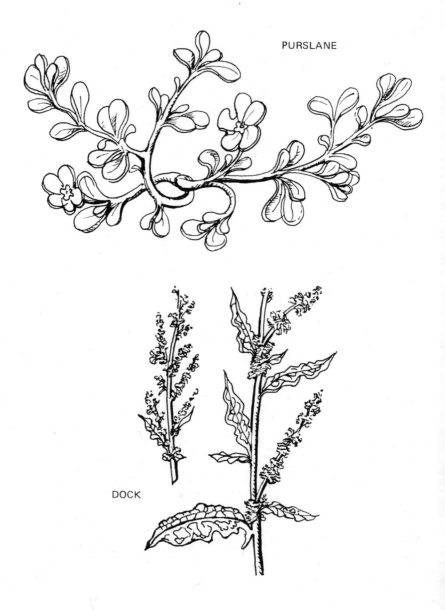

PURSLANE

DOCK

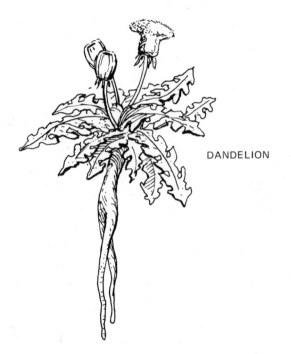

DANDELION

MUSHROOMS

As mentioned at the beginning of this chapter, all mushrooms are better left alone unless you are sure of their identity. Although many mushrooms are edible and offer a good source of food, others are deadly poison.

The most widespread of the dangerous poisonous mushrooms are the *amanitas.* These can be recognized by a frill (called the veil) around the upper part of the stem, and a bag (volva) at the bottom. They also have a white spore deposit that drops out of the gills. The deadly amanitas almost always grow on the ground in the woods or shade.

Puffballs have a somewhat globular body and solid white flesh inside when they are young. All puffballs are edible when fresh. They are especially good tasting fried.

Morel mushrooms are easily recognizable because of the spongy appearance of their heads. There are several varieties of the morel—all edible and all tasty.

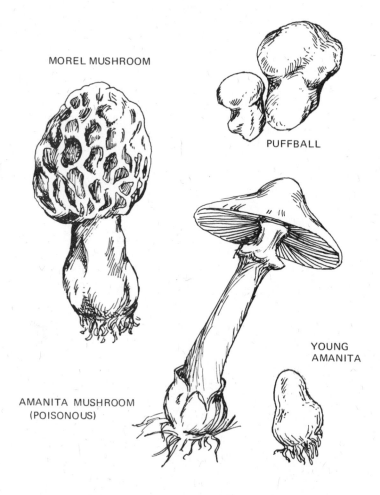

MOREL MUSHROOM

PUFFBALL

YOUNG AMANITA

AMANITA MUSHROOM (POISONOUS)

BARK

In a pinch, food value can be gotten from eating the barks of various trees, either raw or cooked. For eating purposes, the thin green outer bark and the white innermost bark are the best bets, since brown bark usually contains too much foul-tasting tannin to get down. Some of the trees whose bark can be used for food are poplars, birches, willows and some species of pine.

PLANT BEVERAGES

Some plants that have little food value when eaten can be used to make refreshing beverages. A palatable drink can be made by boiling or steeping the bark from sassafrass roots, black birch, spice bushes and wintergreen or mint leaves.

14 The Incompleat Angler

Although wild plant food is plentiful and will help keep you alive, the food value of many edible plants is questionable. Generally, more nourishment can be gotten from animal food. In most cases the readiest source of animal food in the wilderness is fish. And often the deeper into the wilderness you are, the easier the fishing is. Sometimes fish can be caught with a crude spear or even by hand as they head up the creeks on their spawning runs. And with only primitive tools it is possible to put together a serviceable fishhook, line and bait.

Because of this, your chances of survival when lost or stranded are far better if you can find a body of water. This can provide you with a reservoir of food if you know a few rules about when, where and how to fish.

About the only time you will catch a fish with bait is when the fish are feeding. Feeding times vary widely for different species of fish, but in general the best times to fish are in the early morning and late afternoon. Signs that tell you the fish are feeding are jumping minnows and rising fish.

As any fisherman will tell you, if you don't know where to fish, your efforts are wasted. A shallow stream is usually an easier place to locate fish than in a deeper stream, a river or a lake where the fish has much more room to evade you. When you scan the water for fish, look away from the sun or the reflections will make it impossible for you to see below the surface.

In a stream, the most likely place for fish will be in deep, calm water or pools. Some promising places to check are in the shade of overhanging bushes, where there are deep undercut banks, at the head of small rapids, eddies below rocks or logs, and wherever you see submerged logs or rocks. When the main stream or river is high or muddy, the mouth of a small tributary stream is a spot where fish often congregate.

In hot weather when the streams are low, fish will most likely be in the deepest pools and wherever cool underground water enters the main stream. This is also the time when fish will most likely be found hiding under rocks. In the cool weather of spring or fall, fish will spend more time in the shallow water that is warmed by the sun.

A good place to start looking is in the shallows and small feeder streams where there might be spawning fish or schools of fingerlings that can be easily caught. One way to trap a number of fish in pools is by making a small dam of rocks to divert a shallow stream. Fish that are spawning in the shallow water often can be easily caught by hand or speared. At night fish can be lured into easy spearing range by holding a flashlight or torch over the water. This method of fishing is illegal in most places, but the law is not designed to keep a lost camper from spearing fish for his survival.

Any open mesh fabric placed on a forked stick can serve as a dip net to scoop out quantities of minnows. These little fellows can be cooked and eaten whole without the bother of cleaning them.

A fairly simple fish trap can be built in a stream or lake by a person who expects to be stranded there for a considerable time. This can be done by driving stakes into the lake or stream bottom to form a fenced-off area with a narrow funneled opening on one end. The fish that swim in through the small opening hardly ever catch on that they could swim back out the same way, and will stay corralled until you want them. They should, incidentally, be left in the trap alive until they are needed, as fish will spoil rapidly if they are left lying around in weather above freezing.

In looking for bait to catch fish, try the water first, since that is the fish's natural feeding grounds. Some good choices for bait are crayfish, small minnows, fish eggs, small frogs, toads, salamanders or the meat of shellfish. Insects are good too. The well-known earthworm can be found by tipping over rocks or digging in rich, moist soil. Insects with bulky bodies like grasshoppers, locusts, and dragonflies can be found in brush or reeds. A rotten log can yield fat wood grubs, which many fish find irresistible. Chunks of animal meat can make good bait, as can the intestines, eyes and flesh of other fish.

If you are using live bait, try to make it look natural to the fish. Conceal the hook as best you can, and don't let the bait remain still, but move it slowly now and then. If fish are feeding near the surface, let the bait drift with the current.

When you see several fish breaking water and feeding, drop the bait in upstream and let it drift down to them. If you try to plunk it into the middle of a feeding school the fish are likely to be frightened away.

If you have no natural bait, an artificial lure can be fashioned out of bits of white or colored cloth that may tempt a fish, especially if you keep it in motion. Bits of feathers, fur and shiny metal tied to a hook can be effective lures. When a fish takes one of these, you will have to yank on the line quickly. A fish may swallow a piece of natural bait, but he will spit out an artificial lure as soon as he finds he has been deceived.

A workable fishhook can be made out of metal, bone, hard wood, seashell or any other tough material that you can work with a knife or other simple tool. The simplest improvised hook to make is the straight-line gorge hook. This consists of a straight piece of tough material sharpened to a point on both ends with a notch in the middle for tying it to the line. The bait used should be large enough to cover most of the gorge hook. When the fish has taken the bait or, better still, swallowed it whole, a hefty yank will sink one of the gorge hook's two points into him long enough for you to pull him out of the water.

Another kind of fishhook can be made from the fork of a dead branch. Whittle the smaller branch to a sharp point to form the barb. Green wood will not work as well because it is too pliable.

Some bones can be carved into a fairly efficient hook shape. The wishbone of a bird is especially suitable for this purpose. Also, a sharp thorn securely tied to a thin shaft makes an adequate hook.

Any little bits of wire or metal in your equipment or clothing that can be bent and sharpened into a hook shape will work. Wire buckles, for instance, are good for shaping into usable hooks. Don't worry about a barb on your hook since in survival fishing the object is to hoist the fish out of the water as fast as possible. Never mind "playing" him.

The size of your improvised hook should suit the size of the fish you're after. It should be large enough to hook the fish well, but not larger than he will readily swallow.

Often fish gathered in a deep hole that will not bite at a baited hook can be caught by snagging. This involves lowering a series of sharp hooks to the bottom, then jerking them sharply upward.

A good rig for snagging can be made from a stiff sapling about six feet long with a stout line the same length as the pole tied to the end. Tie half a dozen sharp hooks to the line, spacing them about two inches apart, and positioning them so they point away from the line. Hold the line over a deep hole and let the sinker carry it to the bottom. At regular intervals jerk the line up sharply, moving the pole around to cover more area. If the water is clear enough for you to see the fish, maneuver the line beneath them, then give it an upward jerk so that the line snaps against the fish.

In shallow water, spearing can be a more effective way of catching fish than using a hook and line. A spear with a metal point or barb is best. This can be improvised from a large nail or other piece of metal that can be hammered and filed into a sharp point. A sapling can be used for the spear handle, and the point lashed tightly to the handle, preferably with wire, or with leather thongs that will shrink and tighten when wet.

If a metal point for a spear is not available, a dead branch or sapling can be whittled into a point. Green wood is usually too soft to make a good spear point, but some kinds can be hardened by scorching them in a fire.

Any person in the wilderness is almost certain to have some kind of material on him that can be fashioned into a fishing line. Fish that are far from civilization are ignorant in the ways of fishermen, and a thick or crude line will not alarm them as much as it would their more sophisticated brothers who must be tricked with near-invisible factory-made lines.

If you are carrying no string or cord of any kind, search your clothing and equipment for some spare piece of fabric that can be unraveled into thread or cut into strips and braided into a stout line. A patch of leather can be fashioned into a fishing line by cutting in a spiral pattern beginning at the outer edge. Strips of tough plastic will work too.

There are a number of plant fibers that can be used to make an impromptu fishing line. The best is the inner bark from a tree which yields long, tough fibers. A fishing line twenty feet long can be made from braided plant fibers in an hour or so.

If possible, it is a good idea to preserve some of a catch for future use, since freshly caught fish will spoil in a hurry without refrigeration. The handiest way to do this is by smoking the moisture out of the fish.

To smoke a fish, clean it, remove the head, and split the fish up the middle, leaving enough flesh to act as a hinge so you can hang the fish lengthwise across a pole. A long pole to hold the fish should be suspended about four feet above a smoky fire. The heat of the fire should be kept very low, and if possible resinous evergreens should not be used. Adding green wood to the fire will keep the smoke going. To speed up the job, a tent of some kind rigged over the fish will hold the smoke in and keep rain and dew out. The smoky fire should be kept going steadily for one to two days until the fish has a dry and crumbly texture. The length of time it will take depends on the size of the fish and how much dampness there is in the air. When a smoked fish is thoroughly cured it will keep in a cool, dry container for months.

It should be remembered that when you are fishing for survival you are not limited to a single line. You can drop as many baited hooks as you can rig up and then tie the lines to flexible saplings or other anchor points on the shore. The bait on these set lines should be dropped into deep holes for best results.

On a fairly narrow stream you can string a heavy line all the way across and tie your baited set lines to this at intervals. The ends of the cross line should be anchored to a springy young tree or bush flexible enough to take the shock of a heavy fish hitting one of your hooks.

Set lines can safely be left unattended while you sleep or take care of some other business. Few fish, once they are hooked, will escape.

Set-line fishing is another method that is against the law in many areas. However, a man who is lost or stranded need not worry too much about being arrested.

15 The Reluctant Hunter

Even though your reason for going into the wilderness is not to hunt, some unfortunate accident like getting yourself lost or stranded may force you to go after animals for food in order to survive. This chapter will discuss some of the wildlife you will find edible, and offer a few pointers on how to catch them.

FROGS

Although many frogs make delicious eating, there are a few precautions you should take before sitting down to a meal of frog meat. All frogs should be skinned before eating, since some species secrete a poisonous or irritating fluid from their skins. Frogs that are marked with red or yellow are best left alone altogether.

In warm, temperate climates frogs are not hard to find along the banks of lakes and streams and in marshy areas and swamps. At night frogs can be located by the sound of their croaking and with a light. You should approach slowly until you are close enough to clout them with a stick. Larger frogs can be snagged with a hook and line. When you have stunned a frog, give him the *coup de grace* with a knife blade just behind the head, as they often come to unexpectedly and escape.

Frog legs are a particular delicacy, but the whole body can be eaten.

REPTILES

The idea may not be wildly appealing, but in a survival situation snakes can be another source of food. You can find freshwater snakes in sluggish water and along banks that are rocky, muddy, or covered with vegetation. All of these are edible, and some even taste good.

Land snakes, even the poisonous ones, can be eaten too. However, hunting snakes is not your best bet for getting food in the wilderness, since if one of the poisonous variety gets in the first bite, you are in trouble.

Lizards are somewhat safer to subdue than snakes, and they are found nearly everywhere. They can be clubbed or snared with a loop on the end of a stick. When you have removed the scaly skin, the meat can be broiled or fried. Don't be put off by the ferocious look of some lizards; they can still be delicious. The super-ugly iguana, for instance, tastes much like the white meat of chicken.

Turtles are found in both fresh and salt water and in most land areas of the world. All varieties are edible. Small freshwater turtles can be clubbed on the bank, or they can be grabbed by hand or caught with a hook and line in the water, where they are slow swimmers. If you use the hand grabbing technique, grip the turtle well toward the back end of the shell. For the larger turtles such as snappers, don't grab them at all, as they have a vicious bite.

MOLLUSKS

Mollusks such as snails and mussels can be found in all kinds of water conditions. All of them are edible, but it can be dangerous to eat them raw. Some mollusks carry parasites that can cause serious diseases, or they may be contaminated by polluted water.

Streams and rivers are the best places to look for mollusks. They can be easily picked up by hand or found by feeling around in the mud with your feet.

Shallow water with a mud or sand bottom where the mussels can bury themselves is a good place to hunt them. Mussels can be spotted by the narrow dark slit of their open valve or by the narrow trails they leave in the mud.

CRUSTACEANS

Crabs, lobsters, shrimp, crayfish, and prawns are found in various bodies of fresh water throughout the world. They are all edible, but should always be cooked because some carry parasites that are harmful to man. Those from salt water can safely be eaten raw as long as they are fresh. All crustaceans tend to spoil rapidly.

The crustaceans most frequently found in the waterways of North America are crayfish. These can be scooped out of the water with a dip net or gathered from beds of moss under submerged brush and rocks in streams.

INSECTS

Although the thought is not particularly appetizing, the larvae or grubs of many varieties of insects are edible and nourishing enough to make the difference between staying alive and starving.

The chief advantage of insects as an emergency source of food is their availability. One or another form of insect lives in almost every conceivable habitat. Grubs can be found under the bark of dead trees, in the ground, and in rotten logs. In a pinch they can be eaten raw, but they should be fried or boiled. Grasshoppers should always be cooked because some of them carry harmful parasites. Caterpillars are best left alone, since some of them are poisonous, and many are irritating.

BIRDS AND MAMMALS

One fear you can safely put out of your mind is that you might poison yourself by eating unfamiliar wild meat. No mammals or birds are poisonous to eat. The liver of a polar bear could make you very ill, but that should be well down on your list of things to worry about.

Because birds and mammals are all edible and often quite visible, they are often the first thing that comes to mind as a source of emergency food in the wilds. Unfortunately, birds and mammals are usually the least abundant and hardest to catch of all the live sources of potential food.

The reluctant hunter for food should first go after the lower forms of life such as fish, reptiles, mollusks, crustaceans, and insects. There are a lot more of these around, and they are easier to catch. Once the immediate pangs of approaching starvation have been satisfied, you can start thinking about catching birds and mammals.

SHOOTING GAME

Naturally, the problem of getting food is much simplified for the stranded traveler who has with him a high-powered rifle, a shotgun, or even a .22. A big rifle in the .30/06 class will bring down any game animal in the world with a solid hit in the brain, the neck column, or the chest cavity.

Enough small game can be shot with a .22 rifle or a shotgun to keep a lost man from starving. The .22 should in no way be considered a big-game weapon. There are legends of intrepid sportsmen who have brought down grizzlies with a well placed shot to the brain or heart at close range with a .22. However, the price paid for trying this and missing is too high to justify the gamble.

Aside from any possible danger to the hunter, plunking .22 slugs into the body of a deer or other large animal is needlessly cruel. The small bullets will probably not bring the animal down, but they can cause wounds from which the animal may die painfully days later and miles away.

For collecting game the size of rabbits, the .22 is a good survival weapon. You can also shoot fish with it if they are swimming within a few inches of the surface. When trying this, aim slightly under the fish, as the refraction of light caused by the water makes it appear the fish is higher in the water than he really is. A shot from a high-powered rifle can kill a fish even with a near miss just by the shock of the bullet hitting the water.

The best place to hunt for any game is in the fringe areas where clearings meet dense woods, where brushy foothills flatten into open plains, along natural borders formed by trails or ridges and along the banks of lakes or streams. It is very hard to locate game in a dense forest or a thicket of tall brush. You will have much better luck along the edges.

The best time for hunting game animals is in the early morning or late evening, as those are the times when they do most of their moving around. During the middle part of the day most animals are bedded down or holed up in thick cover.

The greatest advantage a person can have in hunting is to see the quarry before it sees him. Thus, if you wait motionless at a strategic point you will usually get more game than if you were moving around searching. A well-defined game trail or a watering hole are good places to set up an ambush. Another advantage of this method of hunting is that it conserves your energy and will not get you any more confused about directions and possible escape routes.

TRAPPING GAME

Since most people are lost or stranded in the wilderness without guns, other methods must be found for catching game. There are a number of traps and snares that can be made fairly easily with available materials, without the need for complicated tools.

The anchored loop snare is one of the simplest. This is effective for catching rabbits when set up along a well-used runway through the brush. For this kind of snare a loop of heavy twine or light wire is suspended over the rabbit trail from a solid overhead branch or an H-shaped arrangement of stout poles. The loop should be about four inches in diameter, and should hang two or three inches above the ground. The theory is that the rabbit pops his head through the loop when he comes down the trail, then tightens the noose in his efforts to escape.

A somewhat more elaborate version of the loop snare has the other end of the wire or twine tied to the bent-down top of a springy sapling. A cross piece held by a trigger keeps the sapling bent until the rabbit puts his head through the loop and frees the trigger by jerking. The sapling then snaps erect and yanks the rabbit up off the ground and out of the way of predators.

One thing to remember with loop snares, as with all traps, is that placing them at random in the hopes some animal will blunder into them will net you zero. Keep in mind the kind of animal you are after, and place the snare in a spot you have good reason to believe is frequented by that animal. If you use a bait, use the kind of food your quarry naturally eats. Be careful not to disturb the natural surroundings any more than absolutely necessary with your trap.

If a handy sapling is not around for attaching your snare line, you can tie it to a heavy log or rock and run the line over a stout tree limb with the weight set to fall and jerk up the snare when triggered.

Put out as many loop snares as you can along the rabbit trail. This will multiply your chances of catching dinner.

If you find a spot where birds commonly feed, such as a sandbar where ducks like to gather, you can lay out several nooses flat on the ground and run a line from them to a hiding place where you can watch while staying out of sight. When a bird is standing over one of the nooses, you give a yank on the line and, hopefully, the noose pulls tight around the bird's feet.

Deadfall traps work on the principle of a heavy weight that falls down when triggered and crushes the unwary bird or animal that has taken the bait. The weight can be a heavy log or a flat stone tilted at a steep angle. A straight stick can be used as an upright to hold the weight in place. A small flat stone should be placed under the upright to prevent it from sinking into the ground. The bait should be placed on a trigger arranged to dislodge the upright, dropping the weight when the bait is disturbed. Be sure you tie the bait on the trigger before setting the trap to avoid dropping the weight embarassingly on yourself.

The familiar box trap can be effective, but unless you happen to have a fairly sturdy box with you, it is most difficult to make one out of available materials. The principle is similar to the deadfall trap, incorporating the baited trigger and upright. The box trap, however, is designed to capture the animal whole rather than crushing it. If you happen to box some sharp-toothed, energetic animal like a fox or bobcat, getting it out of the trap can be a considerable problem.

HAND-TO-HAND COMBAT

There are not many wild animals that are slow enough or stupid enough for a man to catch and kill by hand. One well-known exception is the porcupine, who rates low in both speed and intelligence. When you find one on the ground or in an easy-to-reach position low in a tree, a porcupine is easily dispatched by bashing it in the head with a club or rock. They can be skinned and dressed without painful quill wounds by starting with an incision on the belly where there are no quills. The meat is nourishing and not bad tasting when roasted, fried, or cut up for a stew.

Before you start thinking that the porcupine is the answer to all your emergency food problems, you had better know that they can be most difficult to find. There are large wilderness regions of North America where porcupines are practically unknown. Even where they are plentiful, you will not exactly be tripping over porcupines. They may not be the brightest animals in the forest, but they usually know enough to get up out of reach in a high tree, or to stay close to a sheltering crack in a cliff or an abandoned burrow.

16 Fire Building

For many centuries fire has been a friend to man. It has kept him warm, cooked his food, dried his clothes, and given him light. However, fire remains a friend only as long as man controls it. Once fire gets out of control it can destroy and kill.

When it is used carelessly, fire, normally useful and necessary, becomes a dangerous force. Hundreds of destructive forest fires are started every year by careless campers and others who fail to follow the rules of the out-of-doors. The character and experience of a true woodsman can be measured by the way he builds and takes care of his campfire.

In some areas it is necessary to have a permit for building a fire. If you need one, it can be had free of charge at most sporting goods stores or from the local headquarters of the forest service or of a national park. The park or forest ranger in your area can also give you a campfire permit. Always make sure before you build a fire that your area is not restricted or closed to fires.

SAFETY FIRST AND LAST

In building a campfire, the first thing to consider before you begin, and the final thing to check before abandoning it is its safety.

Before laying out your fire, clear an area of ground at least six feet in diameter. Dig down far enough to reach solid mineral soil. Never build a fire close to overhanging tree branches.

Once the fire is going, don't leave it unattended, even for a short period of time. Keep a watch for flying sparks. They are a forest fire hazard, and they can burn through tent roofs, sleeping bags, and clothing near the fire.

To put out a fire, the best way is to drown it with buckets of water. If possible, logs that have not burned completely should be dipped in a stream or lake. Covering a fire with dirt or stomping it down is never completely foolproof when the woods are dry in the summertime. Pour water on the fire and stir the ashes until the last wisp of steam disappears.

BASIC THREE-DECK FIRE BUILDING

There are available in various manuals a dozen or so different methods of stacking wood for an open fire to provide heat or cooking facilities. However, the newcomer to the woods can take a tip from veteran outdoorsmen and make do with just two or three simple fire arrangements that will take care of all cooking and heating needs.

The basic three-decker arrangement for any kind of fire consists of, from the bottom up, tinder, light sticks of kindling, and heavier sticks of firewood. When a match is touched to the tinder under the two layers of heavier wood, the fire will start quickly and burn with a strong flame. To get the best results, it is important that the tinder and kindling be of the best-burning material available.

TINDER

For the quick-burning fuel at the base of the campfire, you may have better material along with you than you can find in the woods. Crumpled up paper stuffed under the kindling makes excellent tinder. Waxed paper and wax-treated milk cartons are especially good.

A little lighter fluid or other flammable liquid splashed over the kindling can substitute for the tinder. Be sure to pour on the liquid fuel *before* you touch a match to the fire, as these can be highly explosive.

A good natural tinder can be made from the dry dead branches lying under pine or fir trees. Birch bark torn into strips and loosely wadded has enough pitch in it to burn as tinder either wet or dry. Dry cedar bark is another that makes a good tinder. Sage brush, whether it is dead or green, will light and burn easily, especially the shaggy bark. Another fast-lighting tinder is a handful of dry grass or weeds crushed loosely into a wad.

Hard, pitchy sections of dead wood can be found in some half-rotted evergreen logs. Such pitch-filled woods can be recognized by the amber or yellow color of the pitch and the strong smell of resin. Slivers shaved off these pitch chunks are another fine tinder, and will light even when wet.

One standard woodsman's method of getting a fire started is to use a fuzz stick. To make a fuzz stick, a knife or ax is used to shave strips on a stick of dead wood, leaving one end of each shaving attached to the stick. A pair of these propped against each other with the shavings at the bottom will start burning readily.

KINDLING

Thin dry sticks of wood for kindling should be used to loosely cover the tinder in criss-cross or teepee fashion. Wood split from a solid dead tree makes the best kindling. Dead limbs and twigs will do too if they are not more than half an inch thick.

The best source for kindling and all firewood, if you can find one, is a standing dead tree. These provide better fuel than trees that have fallen because constant exposure to wind and sun has dried them out thoroughly. If you find one of these of a size you can handle, cut it down and your firewood problems will be solved.

HEAVIER FIREWOOD

When the tinder and kindling are in place, five or six chunks of fairly heavy firewood can be leaned or stacked over the top. These should be about four inches thick to keep the fire strong and steady. The best firewood comes from branches or small logs chopped to the length you want and split with an ax or hatchet. Split wood burns faster and hotter. For a longer-lasting, warming fire use unsplit logs and branches.

You should gather and cut all the wood you will need to cook your meal and for your warming campfire before you light it. Enough kindling for the breakfast fire should be put aside in a safe, dry place.

All wood does not burn equally well. Some, like white ash, will light quickly and burn well even when green with spring leaves. Others, like alder, can seem to be almost fireproof.

In general, hard woods make a hotter, longer-lasting fire than soft woods. Hard woods will also provide a better bed of coals.

Trees growing in swampy ground do not usually burn as well as those on a ridge where they are exposed to the wind. Not many trees burn well when they are green and alive. If you must use green wood for fuel, it will work better in the fall or winter when there is less sap in it. A drawback of using evergreen trees for fuel is that their resin content causes them to do a lot of snapping and popping, throwing out sparks.

The following is a list of some common trees rated for their suitability for use as firewood:

Good	Fair	Poor
Ash	Beech	Alder
Oak	Sycamore	Willow
Dogwood	Tamarack	Magnolia
Birch	Cedar	Chestnut
Maple	Pine	Catalpa
Hickory	Juniper	Cherry
Holly	Fir	White Elm
Apple	Spruce	
Locust	Cottonwood	
	Aspen	

STARTING THE FIRE

When the tinder, kindling, and firewood have been laid in three decks, a match should be touched to the bottom of the tinder on the upwind side. This will take the flame of the match in and up through the tinder to give the best ignition. Once the tinder has started to burn, the fire can be coaxed along by fanning it or blowing on it.

One simple type of fire can furnish both heat and light, and also provide a supply of hot coals for cooking. The first step in laying this all-purpose fire is to arrange rocks in two rows from four to six feet long, and about one foot apart. This forms an open-fire cooking trench. The fire should be started in the middle of the trench. When the fire has burned down to a bed of coals, a stick can be used to push all the still-burning chunks of wood down to one end of the trench. The fire can then be kept going down there out of the way of the cooking area, and used to replenish the coals as needed. The coal bed provides the low, steady heat that is best for camp cooking. It is nearly impossible to cook properly over a blazing open fire.

If there are not enough rocks available to build the trench, a couple of green logs laid side by side a foot apart will serve. If logs are used instead of rocks, they should not be put in place until after the fire has burned down to coals. Otherwise, the flames will eat the logs away. Since logs do not allow as much side ventilation as rocks, they may have to be propped up from time to time if the coals show signs of dying.

WET WEATHER FIRE BUILDING

The most important thing about starting a fire in the rain or snow is to be methodical about making the preparations. A hurried attempt to get a fire going in wet weather is almost surely doomed to failure. If water is standing on the ground you will need a foundation of rocks or broken limbs for the fire. In snow country, don't build a fire under a tree with snow-laden branches. As the heat from the fire rises, enough of the snow on the branches can be melted to dump the rest down on you and your fire.

Wood split from the center of a standing dead tree will be dry enough to burn in a rainstorm. Don't worry about the wetting it gets while you're doing the splitting—it won't be enough to affect the burning. Dead evergreen branches with good pitch pockets will also burn in the wet. Other fuels that can be counted on to burn even when wet are birchbark and finely split white ash.

If possible, lay out the wet-weather fire under a natural overhang like a rock ledge. If there is no natural shelter from the rain, rig up some kind of a small roof for your fire using a canvas tarp or poncho, or even a flat rock or log propped up to give some measure of protection.

Get together a good supply of tinder, kindling, and heavier firewood and put it in as sheltered a place as you can find. When you are ready to light the fire, be sure you have a dry surface to strike the match on. If you have a candle, light it with the match and use the candle flame to light the tinder.

If the improvised roof over the fire is leaking, lean across to shield the fire with your body while lighting it. Keep the fire shielded as well as you can until the chunks of heavier firewood are blazing. Once they are burning well you can add more pieces of firewood, propping them teepee style on the outside of the fire.

FIRE BUILDING WITHOUT MATCHES

If, heaven forbid, you are caught out with no matches and you must have a fire, there are a number of ways of starting one—none of them very much fun.

Sparks struck by a hard steel object like the back of a knife blade from a piece of flint, quartz, or pyrite can be used to start a fire if the sparks are dropped onto super-dry tinder. Once the tinder catches fire, the flames can be encouraged by blowing on them gently.

Sunlight focused through a glass onto a pile of tinder will start a spark that can be fanned into flame. For the glass you can use the lens of a flashlight, camera, or binoculars. The lens should be held to focus the tiniest pinpoint of light possible to concentrate the heat.

Rubbing two sticks together, the familiar boy scout method, is harder than it sounds. You need completely dry, well-seasoned wood to have a fighting chance of success. Soft-grained woods are usually better for this purpose than hard woods. Any piece of wood with resin in it is useless. The best kinds of woods for starting a fire by friction are elm, willow root, and cottonwood.

The wood-friction method of fire starting can be some-what simplified by the use of a bow and drill. When you spin a shaft of dry, soft wood into a block of the same material, it will form a powdery dust that will begin to smoke, and eventually spark into flame.

Needless to say, no camper wants to spend a lot of his time rubbing pieces of wood together or knocking sparks off a hunk of flint to get a fire going. Keep this thought as a reminder to always carry plenty of waterproof matches in a waterproof case.

17 Outdoor Cooking

It is often said that food cooked out in the woods tastes a whole lot better than the same thing prepared at home with all the modern kitchen conveniences. Whether or not this is literally true, some tasty and nourishing meals can be prepared outdoors by following a few basic rules.

Outdoor cooking should not be expected to provide gourmet meals. The best recipes are those that do not call for a big variety of ingredients or complicated procedures. Whether you are cooking outdoors by design and have carried food in with you, or find yourself on the trail in a living-off-the-land situation, there are four basic methods of cooking over an open fire—frying, boiling, broiling and baking. These methods are enough to prepare almost anything you will want to eat in camp.

FRYING

Many of the foods you eat in camp, especially meats, can be prepared most quickly and easily by frying. There are three methods of outdoor frying, depending on the kind of meat you're cooking.

1. *Plain Frying:* Put a tablespoon of grease in a heavy skillet and heat it until the grease smokes slightly. Fry the meat by first searing it on both sides, then turning it less frequently. For frying vegetables, cut them into small pieces and stir them frequently so they are cooked evenly. Half an inch is a good thickness to slice the meat. Don't cover the skillet while the food is frying, as this will trap moisture inside and give the food a boiled effect.

For frying bacon, start with a cold pan; for frying cured ham, start with a moderately hot one. Eggs are less likely to stick to the pan, and are easier to digest when you fry them over a low heat.

2. *Sautéing:* This method is good for cuts of meat that you like rare or medium-rare. Heat the skillet until it smokes, then rub a piece of bacon over the bottom, but add no more grease. Sear the meat quickly on both sides, seasoning it with salt and pepper before the first turning, and again before you turn it the second time. When the meat is well seared, put the pan over a lower heat and let it cook for a minute or two longer. Keep an eye on the meat you're sautéing, because it has a tendency to stick to the pan, and you will have to loosen it with a fork or spatula.

3. *Pan Roasting.* This method is good for tougher meats. Brown both sides of the meat in a hot greased pan, then add ¼ cup of hot water and cover the pan tightly. From time to

time add more water to keep the meat from sticking.

The fats left in the pan after frying meat can be used to make gravy simply by adding water until you get the thickness you like. In the case of pan roasting there will be mixed grease and water in the pan. To make smooth gravy from this, prepare a paste of flour and cold water before stirring it into the pan.

BROILING

The foods most suitable for broiling outdoors are fish and steaks. To broil a good sized fish, remove the head and split the fish down the back. Spread it flat on a greased grill and sear quickly on both sides in an open flame. Then move the grill over a bed for moderately hot coals. Small fish can be impaled on sharp green branches and held over coals. They should be turned steadily to cook evenly on all sides. Fish should not be overcooked or they will become dry and tough. Usually, five to ten minutes is enough cooking time.

Only lean, tender meat should be broiled. The steaks should be at least one inch thick. Sear the meat quickly on both sides in an open flame, then move it over a bed of hot coals. Broil the steak over the coals according to the following chart.

Thickness	Minutes to Broil	
	Rare	Medium
1 inch	5	6
1¼ inches	8	10
2 inches	15	17

Broiling meat until well done is not recommended. The results can range from poor to inedible. Broiled meat and fish should be seasoned just before serving.

BOILING

Fresh meats should be boiled about fifty minutes for each pound. They should be boiled vigorously for the first five minutes, then more gently until they are done. Boiled meat should be seasoned just before serving.

To make a stew, start with cold water and cook chunks of meat until they are almost done. Then add the carrots and onions, which take about thirty minutes to cook. A little later add the potatoes, which cook in about twenty minutes. The boiling of the stew can be speeded up by adding salt to the water. If you like, the meat can be browned in hot fat before boiling.

BAKING

Baking in camp is usually reserved for breads and biscuits. However, meats and vegetables can be baked too if you like them that way. The baking can be done in a Dutch oven, a covered skillet, or a reflector baker.

Determining the baking temperature can be a problem without an oven thermometer. One practical method is to put a pinch of white flour on a can lid and set it inside the heating oven. After five minutes, check the color of the flour.

If it is light brown, the oven is slow (about 300 degrees), if it is golden brown, the oven is moderate (about 350 degrees), if it is dark brown the oven is hot (400 to 450 degrees).

IMPROVISATION

In cooking outdoors you will often have to make some compromises with what is called for in recipes. For instance, where the recipe specifies fresh milk, either diluted canned milk or dry milk mixed with water will do. Dehydrated vegetables can be substituted when fresh ones are not available. For cooking purposes, bacon fat can take the place of butter. When lemon juice is called for and you don't have it—use vinegar. If some special seasoning other than salt and pepper is specified and you don't have any—leave it out and don't worry about it. It will taste good anyway. Ready-mixed flours that need only the addition of milk or water and sometimes an egg are preferred for outdoor cooking to flours that must be blended with baking soda or baking powder and shortening.

TELLING WHEN IT'S DONE

There is no timer attached to your cooking fire to tell you when the food is done, but it is not too difficult to find out. For boiled or baked meat and vegetables, punch them with a fork. If the tines slide in easily, the food is ready to eat. Beans, rice, and cereal grains should be cooked until they are soft. With bread or cake, stick a splinter of wood into the center. If the splinter comes out with no dough clinging to it, the food has baked long enough.

COOKING AT HIGH ALTITUDES

A longer cooking time is usually required at higher altitudes because water boils at a lower temperature. For this reason the water must boil for a longer time to properly cook the food.

COOKING CANNED FOOD

To cook food in the cans, submerge the can in a kettle of cold water, place the kettle over heat, and bring it to a boil. When the water boils the canned food is ready to eat.

Be careful in opening the hot can. Hold it in a cloth to protect your hand, and make a small puncture in one end to let the steam escape before opening it. The hot water in which you heated the cans can be saved and used later to wash the dishes.

18 Physical Hazards

Even when plenty of food and water are available, there are physical hazards in the wilderness that do not exist in the city. Knowing what the hazards are, and knowing how to avoid or overcome them, increases the odds in favor of a person getting safely back home.

The simple advice, "be careful," cannot be overstressed for the outdoorsman. A small accident like a twisted ankle or a cut from a knife or ax blade, which would be annoying back in civilization, can be deadly in the wilds. Obviously, it pays to be extra alert for safety hazards that you would hardly give a thought to back home.

Many inexperienced campers get into trouble by over-extending themselves. A lot of physical energy is expended in merely hiking through the woods. A newcomer should bear in mind the shape he's in and be careful not to attempt to go too far, too fast, or too high.

SUNBURN

It is much easier to prevent sunburn than to treat it. The sun's burning rays can be warded off by protective clothing such as a long-sleeved shirt, full-length trousers, and a broad-brimmed hat. A coating of protective lotion is good too.

Too often sunburn is thought of as something that happens at the beach, not in the woods or the mountains. However, it is the same sun, and at higher elevations the ultraviolet rays that do the damage are stronger and more intense.

Many people are seriously burned because they don't realize that the effects of sunburn are often not felt until hours after the exposure. If you wait until your skin turns pink or starts to feel hot, it's too late to cover up. Hazy and overcast days can be the worst, because hikers are liable to feel a false sense of security as long as the sun is invisible. However, the droplets of water in the air reflect and magnify the sun's rays, and you can get a painful burn without suspecting it.

HEAT STROKE, SUNSTROKE, AND HEAT EXHAUSTION

The main cause of heat stroke, sunstroke, or heat exhaustion is the loss of the body's salt through perspiration. Salt tablets, which can be purchased in any drugstore, are a good way to prevent these maladies. In a humid, tropical climate the sweating is obvious enough to make you aware of your need for salt. However, in a hot, dry climate perspiration evaporates so fast you may not even know it. The body also loses ascorbic acid through sweating. This can be replenished by eating citrus fruits.

Sunstroke is caused by prolonged direct exposure to the sun. It may strike you down suddenly, but usually it is preceded by headache, dizziness, and nausea. The face feels flushed and the skin hot and dry. Keeping the head covered is the best way to guard against sunstroke. It also helps to drink plenty of water and take extra salt.

Heat exhaustion can occur without direct exposure to the sun. It can be the result of a prolonged period of exertion in high-humidity heat. The skin becomes clammy and the body temperature may fall below normal. The best way to avoid heat exhaustion is simply to take it easy when it's hot, drink water, and take your salt.

SNOW BLINDNESS

A constant exposure to the rays of the sun reflected off snow can produce the painful inflammation of the inner side of the eyelids known as snow blindness. The effects can range from a slight irritation to a temporary blindness that lasts several days. The best prevention for snow blindness is dark glasses or goggles. Lacking glasses, you can reduce the effects of the glare by blackening your eyelids, cheeks, and the bridge of your nose, or fashioning a dark mask with narrow eye slits.

FROSTBITE

A constant danger in temperatures below freezing is frostbite—the local freezing of hands, feet, and face. Frozen flesh becomes stiff and white. Milder cases of frostbite turn the skin a dark red.

Never rub the frozen parts or expose them immediately to heat. Rubbing will scrape the skin away and leave a raw area open to infection. The frozen parts should be thawed slowly.

While traveling in icy weather, wrinkle your face continually to feel if any part of it is freezing. The ears are especially vulnerable to frostbite. Cup your warm hands against your ears now and then to warm them up.

If your fingers show signs of becoming frostbitten, warm them against the bare skin of your body. Feathers, moss, or dry grass placed in your shoes for insulation will help protect your toes. A cloth mask tied below the eyes and allowed to hang loosely will protect your face and allow your moist breath to escape.

The danger of frostbite increases greatly when you are traveling in a cold wind. A sixty-mile-an-hour wind at a temperature of zero feels colder and does more harm than calm weather at fifty degrees below zero. This is because the heat of the body is snatched away by the wind. When the wind blows in cold weather, take a tip from the animals and head for shelter.

MOUNTAIN SICKNESS

The lack of oxygen at higher altitudes, intensified by physical exertion, can cause symptoms of weakness, headache, dizziness, and nausea in a person not accustomed to the altitude. Mountain sickness is best prevented by setting a slow pace and making frequent short stops. Any sign of mountain sickness will only be made worse by heavy exertion, chilling, or drinking cold water when you are hot and tired.

BURNS

Painful burns around the campfire and hot cooking utensils can be avoided by using pot holders or wearing inexpensive cotton work gloves.

SOAPY DISHES

Dishes that have not been properly rinsed after washing can retain a film of soap suds. Eating from these soapy dishes is liable to cause diarrhea. Rinsing the dishes in scalding water will cleanse them of soap and sterilize them.

CONTAMINATED FOOD

Never eat food from a can you have packed that has become punctured or developed a bulge. The food inside is very likely spoiled, and can be dangerous to eat.

CUTS

All cutting tools such as axes, hatchets, hunting knives, and camp saws should have leather or canvas guards over the cutting edge to prevent injury. A serious offender in causing cuts and puncture wounds is the old-fashioned pointed can opener. If you still have one of these old timers, get rid of it and buy one of the models with a twist handle.

WATER HAZARDS

Streams of all sizes can present special problems when you have to cross them. A shallow, swift-moving stream can be crossed using a stout pole as a brace to help you keep your balance. If the bottom has poor footing because of rocks, and the current is moving slowly, you can cross by keeping most of your body submerged to take the weight off your feet. Deep streams with swift currents are best crossed by swimming diagonally downstream.

If the stream is wide, or if you are not a strong swimmer, use a log or a small raft to help float you across. If the water is cold, take something to hang on to, no matter how good a swimmer you are. Icy water can rapidly numb your arms and legs.

If you must cross thin ice, lie down to distribute your weight and push yourself along. If you fall through a hole, don't try to climb out. Stretch out both arms along the surface of the ice and kick your legs vigorously to bring your body up level. Then "swim" out onto the solid ice and roll to a safe place.

QUICKSAND

Quicksand is sand that is held in suspension by water. Patches of quicksand look very much like ordinary sand, and are found near the mouths of large rivers, along silt-laden rivers with shifting water courses, and on flat shores. If a suspicious area has pebbles lying on it, it is probably not quicksand. If you are not sure about a patch of sand you can test it by throwing a small stone on it. If the stone sinks, it's quicksand, and you would be wise to take a detour.

If you feel yourself sinking in quicksand or a bog of any kind, fall forward, spread out your arms, and start to swim or pull your way along. Struggling or trying to lift your feet while in an upright position will only make you sink deeper. Move slowly, and keep your lungs full of air for buoyancy. Even a fair swimmer can make his way through miles of bog this way, as long as he keeps calm.

CLIFFS

If you have to climb up or down a cliff, there are a number of techniques that can make it easier and safer:

1. Don't put your weight on any hold before testing it.

2. Keep your weight distributed on two or more points. Keep your feet wide apart when standing.

3. Don't try to climb on rotten or loose rock.

4. Keep moving. A continuous movement from one hold to the next conserves your strength.

5. Use your legs to provide the lifting power, and your hands mostly for balance.

6. When coming down a steep incline, keep your face, not your back to the cliff.

19 Animal Hazards

Chances are very slight of anyone in the woods suffering personal injury from a wild animal. Most of them instinctively avoid man, and many species are so timid you are never likely to see one. Nevertheless, it should be remembered that they *are* wild animals, and even the friendly ones in the national parks should be treated with respect. Also, there are a few marauders that can do damage to a camp if you are not prepared to cope with them.

BEARS

Bears are most likely to be seen in the campgrounds of national parks like Yosemite, Yellowstone, and Grand Teton. The rules in these parks are very explicit—don't feed or molest the bears. In spite of this, every year hundreds of people break the rules. Most of them are lucky, but a few wind up in the hospital.

The kind of bear usually encountered in the national parks is the common black bear. They are not notably ferocious, even in the wilds where they have not been pampered and protected, but in certain circumstances they can be as dangerous as the unpredictable grizzly.

If you meet a bear on the trail or in a campground, the best procedure is to walk slowly away. The bear might be frightened into an attack by any sudden movement on your part.

It is an excellent practice to stay away from bear cubs, no matter how cute they are. If you happen to get between the cubs and their mother, you are asking for an attack.

If a bear somehow gets you cornered and actually seems to be menacing you, grab a stout stick or some other weapon and advance slowly. That should be enough to drive it off.

Actually, bears are much more likely to tear up your camp than they are to go after your person. A combination of hunger and curiosity will bring bears into a camp at night or when it is unattended. A bear's way of investigating things is to chew them up a little bit, and he can make quite a mess of things before his curiosity is satisfied.

A light wooden box is no protection for food against a hungry bear. Their powerful teeth and claws can make instant splinters of such containers. One sure way of keeping your food safe is to put it in a sack and suspend it from a tree limb out of the reach of bears.

PORCUPINES

The main threat posed by a porcupine is that it will chew up a good deal of your equipment. The porcupine is attracted by salt, and will gnaw on anything that tastes of human perspiration, such as ax handles, canoe paddles, and boots. However, if you are unlucky enough to frighten or anger one of these walking pincushions, he may slap at you with his tail. If he makes contact, this will leave a number of barbed quills stuck painfully in your skin.

Once porcupines have decided your camp is to their liking, they can be very hard to discourage. As many times as you chase these slow-witted creatures away, they will probably come trundling back within a few minutes. Better to keep anything with a salt taste out of their reach.

RACCOONS

Raccoons, though they may be cute little devils, are capable of doing a great deal of damage to tent fabric and containers if they are attracted by the smell of food. However, they are easily scared off by a thrown rock or a good yell.

SKUNKS

Skunks are well-mannered, playful, and rather charming creatures, except for their one terrible weapon. Also, they are practically fearless and don't hesitate to walk into an occupied tent if there is food available. If a skunk does stroll into your tent, the best thing to do is sit tight, affect an air of cordial indifference, and let him do whatever he had in mind until he is ready to leave and wanders out. If you make him feel threatened in any way, a skunk will fire off his malodorous spray, which can be more than enough to ruin a camping trip.

SNAKES

Man has an instinctive fear of snakes and snakebite that is all out of proportion to the facts. In the United States there are some 300 varieties of snakes. Only four of these are poisonous. They are the rattlesnake, the coral snake, the copperhead, and the water moccasin or cottonmouth. These four are dangerous, but they are shy creatures who will help you avoid them by staying out of sight if they possibly can. Fewer people die every year from snakebite than from being struck by lightning.

The two situations in which snakebites most often occur are in hiking, when a hiker inadvertently steps on or near a snake, and in climbing on steep rocky slopes. It pays to know where you're putting your foot down, especially in rocky, hilly terrain.

Only the rattlesnake, of the four poisonous types, is found throughout the United States, and he is rare in the far northeast and north central sections of the country. The copperhead lives in the eastern half of the United States from New England to Texas. The water moccasin is found throughout the southeast in swampy areas. The coral snake lives along the coast in the southeast, and in the deserts of Arizona.

When you are hiking through snake country there are a few good rules you can follow to cut down your chances of being bitten:

1. Stay on the trail, and watch where you step.

2. Wear boots and trousers that cover the boot tops.

3. Don't sit on the ground without taking a good look around first.

4. Cut down traveling at night, since that is when many snakes are most active.

5. Don't reach into any holes or under bushes where you can't see.

6. Be extra careful stepping over logs when you can't see what might be lying on the other side.

7. When climbing above rocky ledges, don't put your hand above you until you can see where you're putting it.

8. Never tease or pick up a strange snake. (Surprising as it may seem, many cases of snakebite result from just this kind of foolish behavior.)

LIZARDS

There are only two known poisonous lizards in the world. Only one of them, the gila monster, is found in the United States. This lizard lives in the desert regions of the southwest, primarily Arizona and Utah.

The gila monster is a ferocious-looking yellow and black creature about eighteen inches long with a blunt nose and tail. However, it is not nearly as fearsome as it looks, and it is not likely to attack you unless you start something. If you are bitten by a gila monster, the prescribed action is to smack him on the nose to break his grip at once, since the lizard's poison is released into the wound slowly as it chews.

20 Battling the Bugs

Far more problems are caused for campers and hikers by insects than by all members of the animal kingdom. Fortunately, there are not many insects in this country capable of causing serious injury or illness, but they can still make your time spent outdoors absolutely miserable.

MOSQUITOS AND FLIES

Mosquitos are likely to be anywhere throughout the United States. Black flies are blood-sucking creatures that show up in the spring and summer in northern forest areas. The fierce-biting deerfly is found in summer in the Rockies and other high country. The tiny biting flies called no-see-ums or midges are everywhere in the woods.

The best defense against these flying pests is to avoid them. This can be done by choosing for your campsite an area unattractive to insects. Such an area would be dry, open ground, preferably with a breeze.

Try to stay away from stagnant water, tall grass, and thick woods. Also, since most of these flying insects are killed off by the first frost of all, it is worth thinking about taking your trip then instead of during the hot summer months.

Loose clothing that is closed at the collar and the wrists will protect most of your body from mosquitos. A head net and unlined leather gloves will take care of the head and hands. A head net is a nuisance to wear, but it can be worth it if the mosquitos are really thick. A point to remember in buying one is that a black or brown net is easier to see through then a white or light colored one.

Rubbing insect repellent on your exposed skin can keep the pests off you for several hours unless it is washed off by sweat or rain. You can add another coating when needed.

An aerosol bug bomb will effectively wipe out mosquitos and their pals in an enclosed space like a tent. They can also be used to clear an eating area before a meal.

A smudge fire can be useful in discouraging mosquitos from buzzing your camp. To keep from also discouraging the campers, you should build your smudge fires in metal cans or buckets and place them about fifty feet upwind from the camp. Green grass or green pine needles laid over a bed of glowing coals makes an excellent smudge. Be sure to set the cans on wet or mineral soil where there is no danger of starting a fire. After the smoke has had a chance to drift through the camp for a while, most of the bugs will go somewhere else.

BEES AND WASPS

If they are left alone, bees and wasps will not usually be a problem to the camper. They have other things on their minds and don't go around stinging people unless they have a reason. Sometimes, of course, a bee will get offended and sting you anyway, even though you meant no harm.

Though a sting can be painful for a little while, it is no particular threat to health unless you are stung by a whole swarm, or are allergic to bee or wasp venom. If you run across one of their nests in the woods, leave it alone.

TICKS

The tick is a flat brown creature about a quarter of an inch long that is found throughout much of the country in wooded or brushy areas. Ticks often take refuge in rotten stumps and old logs and in the burrows of small animals. They are blood-sucking parasites with a bite you can't feel, so they may go unnoticed at first. Rocky Mountain spotted fever is carried by some ticks, but the percentage that are infected is quite small.

There are repellents available that will do a good job of keeping the ticks off you. It is also a good idea to make a regular check of your body and scalp. If you find a tick dug in, covering it with motor oil, mineral oil, or salad oil will shut off its breathing apparatus. If the tick doesn't back out, leave the oil on for half an hour, then remove the tick with tweezers. Be sure to get out all the parts, then wash the area with soap and water.

CHIGGERS

Chiggers, or mites, are found in most regions of the United States where there is thick vegetation. They are so tiny that it is difficult to see them with the naked eye, but their bites can cause considerable itching and irritation. Chiggers often sneak in under tight clothing such as shoes and socks to do their mischief.

A good commercial repellent will keep chiggers off. The discomfort caused by their bites can be relieved by ammonia water, rubbing alcohol, or a baking soda solution.

SCORPIONS

The sting of most scorpions is no worse than that of a bee. The only poisonous scorpion found in this country is along the Mexican border, particularly in Arizona.

Scorpions like to rest up in cool dry places. An example of such a place is your empty shoes. It is a good idea to knock your shoes out in the morning before putting them on.

SPIDERS

The only spider native to the United States that is potentially dangerous is the black widow. It is found throughout the country, but mostly in the southern half. If you get close enough to a black widow you can recognize her by the red mark in the shape of an hourglass on her abdomen. Black widows live in woodpiles, under stones, in decaying logs, and in hollow stumps. Often, they are found in a seldom-used privy. It is wise to brush such facilities out with a stick or a rolled-up newspaper before using them.

21 First Aid

A good working knowledge of first aid is essential to anyone who plans even a short jaunt into the wilderness. When there are no roads or telephones available, you can't depend on the swift arrival of an ambulance or a doctor in case of an emergency. A person in the wilderness has no choice other than to take care of himself or someone else until such time as medical help is available. He should also be able to treat minor illnesses and injuries that may not be serious enough to need a doctor's care, but if untreated could still ruin a camping trip.

FIRST-AID KIT

The following items are considered essential for a first-aid kit to be taken into the woods:

Antiseptic ointment
Burn ointment
Adhesive bandages and tape
Gauze
Scissors
Tweezers for splinters
Aspirin
Bicarbonate of soda
Laxative
Water purification tablets

A kit containing these items can be bought for four or five dollars. If you have a sturdy box at home you can assemble one yourself for less. An added protection for when you go into an area where snakes are plentiful is a snakebite kit.

A good book of first-aid instructions is a must. One of the best and most complete manuals available is the *First Aid Textbook* put out by the American Red Cross.

GENERAL RULES

The following are general instructions, in sequence, for treating anyone who appears to be seriously injured or ill:

1. Keep the injured person lying down so that his head is level with his body while you examine him carefully to determine the seriousness of the injury.

2. Look for, and treat first, the things that can cause immediate death. In order of seriousness they are: bleeding from an artery, stoppage of breathing, poisoning, and shock.

3. Send or signal for help. If you are alone, start a smoky signal fire or fire three rifle shots as a distress signal.

4. Do not give the victim any liquids if there is a possibility of internal injuries. Never pour any liquid into the mouth of an unconscious person.

5. Make the victim as warm and comfortable as possible. Act calm and cheerful to reassure him, and keep sightseers away. Don't let the victim look at a serious wound.

6. Do not move a seriously injured victim unless it is absolutely necessary.

ARTERIAL BLEEDING

Bleeding from an artery can be recognized by the blood pumping out in spurts or welling up strongly. Unless it is treated at once, arterial bleeding is a sure killer.

1. Apply pressure directly on the wound, using the first material that comes to hand as a bandage pad. In this case cleanliness is secondary to stopping the bleeding at once.

2. If the bleeding continues, apply pressure with your fingers at a pressure point that will check the flow of blood to the wound. You should become familiar with the pressure points on the body.

3. As a last resort, apply a tourniquet tightly above the wound. Since a tourniquet can cause the loss of the limb on which it is used, it should not be considered unless there is no other way of stopping the arterial bleeding. Once applied, a tourniquet should be kept tight until it can be removed by a doctor.

STOPPAGE OF BREATHING

There are four common accidents that can cause breathing to stop: drowning, inhalation of smoke or gases, electrical shock, and an obstruction in the throat. In all cases, the victim will be unconscious and not breathing. The lips will be blue, and the face either flushed or pale. The pulse will be weak or absent. In any case where breathing has stopped, the proper treatment is artificial respiration.

A victim felled by shock from an electrical power line must be approached with caution. The electric wire should first be pulled away with a rope or a dry wooden pole. The high voltage shock may have caused serious burns, but these can be treated later. The first consideration is to get the victim breathing again.

For a person choking on some object lodged in his throat, the immediate treatment is to hold him upside down or bend him sharply forward and slap him briskly on the back. If this fails to dislodge the object, try to get it out with your fingers. If breathing stops apply artificial respiration.

ARTIFICIAL RESPIRATION

In giving artificial respiration, the most important thing is to begin immediately. The time spent moving the victim to a more convenient location or waiting for mechanical equipment may cost him his life.

The newer mouth-to-mouth method of artificial respiration is much more effective than the older techniques where the victim lay prone and the rescuer applied pressure to his back or tried to stimulate breathing by lifting the victim's hips or arms. The newer method is simpler to apply and saves many lives. You should not worry about infection, which is unlikely, or waste time trying other methods before getting right to it.

Here are the steps to follow in applying mouth-to-mouth artificial respiration:

1. Turn the victim on his back and remove all foreign matter from his mouth with your fingers.

2. Tilt the victim's head as far back as possible and pull his jaw forward.

3. Open your mouth and place it tightly over the victim's mouth. Pinch his nostrils shut and blow into his mouth.

4. Remove your mouth and listen for the exhalation of air from the victim. Repeat the blowing procedure—about twelve vigorous breaths per minute for an adult, twenty shallower breaths per minute for a child.

5. Keep blowing rhythmically into the victim's lungs until he starts breathing on his own or until medical help arrives.

6. When the victim revives, keep him lying quietly. He can be given warm liquid to drink if he is not nauseated. The victim should rest for twenty-four hours.

POISONING

The symptoms of poisoning are stomach pains, nausea, headache, bloated or flushed face, burns inside the mouth, convulsions, and finally, loss of consciousness.

When the nature of the poison is unknown, use the following treatment:

1. Give the victim all the liquid he can drink to dilute the

poison in his system. A teaspoon of baking soda or salt in warm water or milk is a good mixture. If the poison is a caustic, such as ammonia, milk is the best choice.

2. Try to induce vomiting by tickling the victim's throat with your finger.

If the poison is known to be an acid or alkali, vomiting should not be induced. Rather, the acid or alkali should be neutralized.

For acid poisoning, baking soda, milk of magnesia, or a chalk solution in water are good antidotes. These should be followed with egg whites, olive oil or milk to protect the lining of the digestive tract.

If the poison is an alkali it can be neutralized by drinking a glass of water followed by a mild acid such as vinegar or lemon juice.

SHOCK

Shock is a breakdown of bodily functions caused by other injuries such as broken bones, serious burns, loss of blood, internal injuries, or extreme pain. The symptoms include pale and clammy skin, dull eyes, dilated pupils, shallow and irregular breathing, weak and rapid pulse, faintness and nausea.

Use the following treatment for shock victims:

1. Have the victim lie down flat and cover him with a blanket to prevent shivering.

2. Give him a cup of warm water, milk, coffee or tea unless he is nauseated or unconscious, or unless there is a possibility that he will soon undergo surgery.

3. Get medical help as soon as possible. Shock can kill, even though the injury that brought it on is not fatal.

MINOR EXTERNAL BLEEDING

For bleeding that is not immediately dangerous, take care to guard against infection. It is best, if possible, to wash your hands thoroughly before treating such a wound. The wound should be washed out with soap and water, then covered with a sterile bandage. For small cuts a drop of disinfectant such as iodine, covered by a stick-on bandage of tape and gauze will do the job.

INTERNAL BLEEDING

A heavy blow may cause bleeding internally even when there is no break in the skin. The symptoms are a pale face, weak and rapid pulse, thirst and a feeling of weakness.

1. Have the victim lie flat on his back unless this position hampers his breathing. When necessary, prop him up slightly to make it easier for him to breathe.

2. Be ready to turn his head to one side if vomiting occurs.

3. Keep the victim quiet and try to reassure him by your demeanor.

NOSEBLEED

1. Have the victim sit or lie down with his head back.

2. Hold a finger pressed to the outside of the nostril for about five minutes to give the blood a chance to clot.

3. Apply cold, wet cloths to the face and neck.

4. If bleeding continues pack sterile gauze into the nostrils.

BROKEN OR DISLOCATED BONES

Do not try to set a broken bone or put a dislocated joint back in place by yourself. When in doubt, treat the injury as a fracture. The symptoms are pain and tenderness at the point of the break, often with swelling and discoloration. In a compound fracture the bone breaks through the skin, often causing severe bleeding.

Unless it is absolutely necessary, do not move the victim or the broken limb. If the patient must be moved, immobilize the broken limb with a padded splint. The splint should be long enough to keep the joints above and below the break from moving.

BURNS

For small first- and second-degree burns that redden or blister the skin, apply burn ointment, cover the burned area with sterile gauze, and bandage it snugly.

For third-degree burns where the skin is charred and there is damage to the underlying tissue, treatment by a doctor is essential. You should try to treat such burns yourself only if there is no alternative.

If no professional help is available you should not try to clean the burned area, but cover it with ten or more layers of sterile dressing. Put a snug bandage over the dressings and treat the victim for shock, which is always present in severe burn cases. Have the victim drink as much as he can of a solution of ½ teaspoon of baking soda and 1 teaspoon of salt in a quart of water.

SNAKEBITE

An oft-stated piece of advice for snakebite victims is that they should remain calm. As you may imagine, this is impossible to follow, but there are other things you can do.

1. Have the victim lie down and stay as quiet as possible. This is to slow down his blood circulation and the spread of the venom.

2. If the bite is on an arm or a leg, as most bites are, tie a constricting bandage about three inches above the wound. The bandage should be just tight enough to slow down surface blood flow through the veins, but *not* so tight as to cut off arterial flow. If the limb turns white or blue, the bandage is too tight. Every fifteen or twenty minutes the bandage should be removed for a period of two or three minutes.

3. Sterilize a knife or razor blade by holding it in a flame, and make an "X" cut a quarter of an inch long through each of the punctures. The incisions need be no deeper than the fang punctures, and should be slanted to avoid cutting a tendon or major blood vessel.

4. If the swelling spreads, move the constricting band higher on the affected limb. Make more incisions and apply suction wherever serious swelling and discoloration appear.

6. Give the victim plenty of water to drink. In spite of tradition, whiskey is not recommended.

7. As soon as possible get the victim to a hospital, even if it is hours or days after the emergency first-aid treatment.

BEE STING

To treat a sting by a bee, wasp or hornet, remove the stinger if it is still in the skin, and apply a paste of baking soda and cold cream. Cold packs will numb the pain, and calamine lotion will relieve the itching that follows.

POISON IVY, OAK AND SUMAC

When the skin comes in contact with poison ivy, poison oak or poison sumac it will become red and swollen, break out in small blisters, and itch like crazy. In treating such irritation the affected area should first be washed with soap and water, then sponged with alcohol. Then a heavy paste of melted soap should be applied and left on overnight. After that the itching can be relieved with calamine lotion.

PUNCTURE WOUNDS

Small, deep puncture wounds are always liable to infection. For a person who has not had a recent inoculation, there is the added danger of fatal tetanus or lockjaw. Puncture wounds should be treated as follows:

1. Squeeze the wound lightly to encourage bleeding and flush it out.

2. Apply a sterile pad and bandage.

3. As soon as possible have a doctor clean out the wound and give a tetanus shot if necessary.

4. If the puncture wound was caused by an animal bite, be sure and tell the doctor, as rabies is a deadly possibility.

BLISTERS

If a blister breaks open, wash it with soap and water and cover the raw skin with a sterile bandage. It is best to leave an unbroken blister intact unless it interferes with walking. If a blister must be broken, prick the edge of it with a sterilized blade and force the fluid out. Use a disinfectant and cover it with a sterile bandage.

A-B-C

Keeping informed on the latest techniques of first aid, and carrying with you a standard kit and manual on first aid are essential precautions for heading into the wilds. Most important of all, though, is the A-B-C of woodsmanship—Always Be Careful!

Suggested Reading

American Red Cross. *First Aid Textbook.* Philadelphia.

Boy Scounts of America. *Scout Field Book.* New Brunswick, N.J.

Campground Atlas. Champaign, Ill.: Alpine Geographical Press.

Carhart, Arthur H. *Outdoorman's Cookbook.* Toronto: Macmillan.

Craighead, Frank C. and John J. *How to Survive on Land and Sea.* Annapolis: United States Naval Institute.

Fletcher, Colin. *The Complete Walker.* New York: Alfred A. Knopf.

_____. *The Man Who Walked through Time.* New York: Alfred A. Knopf.

_____. *The Thousand-Mile Summer.* Berkeley: Howell-North Books.

Gibbons, Euell. *Stalking the Wild Asparagus.* New York: David McKay Co.

Kjellstrom, Bjorn. *Be an Expert with Map and Compass.* New York: American Orienteering Service.

McLaren, Peter. *Axe Manual of Peter McLaren.* Philadelphia: Fayette R. Plumb, Inc.

Merrill, W.K. *All About Camping.* Harrisburg, Pa.: The Stackpole Co.

Miracle, Leonard, with Decker, Maurice H. *Complete Book of Camping.* New York: Harper Bros.

Schwartz, Alvin. *Going Camping.* Toronto: Macmillan.

Sportsman's Handbook. Chicago: Science and Mechanics Publishing Co.

Wells, George and Iris. *Handbook on Wilderness Travel.* New York: Harper Bros.

Whelan and Angier. *On Your Own in the Wilderness.* Harrisburg, Pa.: The Stackpole Co.

Other Nash Quality Paperbacks Related to Health and Nutrition You'll Be Sure to Enjoy

THE MAGIC OF HONEY by Dorothy Perlman. The ancients appreciated the glorious taste of honey — symbol of love in story, music and poetry. Health-food enthusiasts have discovered, once again, honey's powers — its delicious flavor, medicinal qualities and natural nutritional values. Here is everything you'd like to know about honey: it's role in history, its wondrous energy- and health-giving attributes, its legendary possibilities as a fertility food and aphrodisiac. #8001 $1.95

ORGANIC MAKE-UP by Mary Gjerde. Whatever your age or skin type, nature provides an aid to protect and enhance your skin. Honey, eggs and milk; plant substances such as herbs, fruits, leaves and seeds; extracts and rich oils of almond, avocado and olive are all natural materials intended by nature for you to use on your skin and hair. And you will find all of these natural ingredients in your own kitchen at a fraction of the cost charged for their synthetic counterparts. #8003 $1.95

VITAMIN E: KEY TO SEXUAL SATISFACTION by Gary P. Brandner. Everyone's talking about Vitamin E. Here is a revealing account of how and why the amazing "E" has come to be known as "the sex vitamin." If a vitamin can be called topical, Vitamin E is just that. The author traces its history and documents how it heightens sexual capabilities and increases response and sensitivity during sexual encounters. #8000 $1.95

INTRODUCTION TO HEALTH FOODS by Marjorie Miller. This complete guide on how to prepare and enjoy health foods introduces the novice to the various types and forms of health foods, their nutritional value, the dangers of artificial preservatives, general principles of good nutrition, how to cook food so it doesn't lose its value, and exactly what foods are found in a health food store. #1187 $2.45

INTRODUCTION TO ORGANIC GARDENING by Chuck Pendergast. The author shows how organic gardening will improve the quality of the foods we eat and help restore the natural balance which has been destroyed by the use of pesticides and chemical fertilizers. Illustrates how to grow your own fruit and vegetables the safe, healthy and natural way. #1188 $2.45

Announcing
a New Solution to the Common Cold
by Dale Alexander:

The Common Cold and Common Sense

Vitamin C is only part of the answer, claims Dale Alexander in this revolutionary work dealing with the common cold. Author of the best seller, Arthritis and Common Sense, Dale Alexander presents a totally new understanding of the common cold, including nutritional secrets that he contends will not only help prevent your catching cold but will ensure your general good health.

This is a book on the common cold which fully recognizes the importance of sound nutrition in combatting the cold. The author introduces you to his original Common Cold-Preventive Cocktail — a new way of eating — which quickly helps to build resistance to the common cold, reduces the length of a cold, and in some instances aborts a cold within a day. He also offers a complete week of daily menus for those who are overweight, underweight and normal weight, which will further help build resistance to the common cold. His menus include recipes for the nourishing Alexander Vegetable and Fruit Salads.

Dale Alexander also offers observations from his years of study and research with doctors and common-cold victims. He contends that certain tempting foods and beverages are partially responsible for the common cold and points out the cold-causing danger of holiday and birthday parties.

If you follow Dale Alexander's sensible, pleasant, nutritional regimen and pay heed to what he claims causes the common cold, the author maintains that the results will be greatly desired good health — free of colds — and the ability to function on all fronts. #1172 $5.95